This book is dedicated to Jess, for her unwavering support and love.

Morgan Kaufmann Publishers is an imprint of Elsevier.
30 Corporate Drive, Suite 400, Burlington, MA 01803, USA

This book is printed on acid-free paper.

Working together to grow
libraries in developing countries
www.elsevier.com | www.bookaid.org | www.sabre.org

ELSEVIER   BOOK AID International   Sabre Foundation

Notices

Knowledge and best practice in this field are constantly
changing. As new research and experience broaden our
understanding, changes in research methods, professional
practices, or medical treatment may become necessary.
Practitioners and researchers must always rely on their
own experience and knowledge in evaluating and using any
information, methods, compounds, or experiments described
herein. In using such information or methods they should be
mindful of their own safety and the safety of others, including
parties for whom they have a professional responsibility.
To the fullest extent of the law, neither the Publisher nor the
authors, contributors, or editors, assume any liability for any
injury and/or damage to persons or property as a matter of
products liability, negligence, or otherwise, or from any use
or operation of any methods, products, instructions, or ideas
contained in the material herein.

Library of Congress Cataloging-in-Publication Data
Application Submitted

British Library Cataloguing-in-Publication Data
A catalogue record for this book is available from the British
Library.

ISBN: 978-0-12-378624-1

For information on all Morgan Kaufmann publications,
visit our website at www.mkp.com or www.elsevierdirect.com

Printed in Canada
09 10 11 12 13   5 4 3 2 1

Production Credits

Writing and Editing: Jon Kolko
Contributed Articles: Chris Connors,
Justin Petro, Uday Gajendar, & Ellen Beldner
Photograpy: Justin Petro. Copyright for various photographs
found within this text held by Justin Petro.
Design, Typesetting: Paul Burke & Justin Petro

About the Book Designers

Justin Petro and Paul Burke are co-founders of Thinktiv.
Thinktiv is a venture accelerator—an ecosystem of people
and technology focused exclusively on business innovation
for brand, marketing, and technology challenges. Learn more
about Thinktiv at www.thinktiv.com.

beginning	15 word	14 natural	13 machine	12 researchers	11 guidelines	11 rhetoric	10 author	10 mapping	9 university	9 values
usable	15 developed	14 professional	13 projects	12 desirable	11 show	11 test	10 definition	10 affordance	9 heart	9 worth
psychology	15 trust	14 pragmatic	13 thoughts	12 program	11 solving	11 technological	10 beautiful	10 functional	9 financial	9 graphic
inquiry	15 creates	14 focused	13 rhetorical	12 play	11 choices	11 written	10 macintosh	10 semiotics	9 family	9 philosophy
success	15 thing	14 convergent	13 signs	12 vivid	11 internal	11 artist	10 dramatic	9 description	9 devices	9 printed
scientists	15 build	14 resources	13 shape	12 daily	11 lives	11 technique	10 control	9 methodology	9 cultures	9 desire
future	15 ask	14 money	13 mindfulness	12 cases	11 popular	11 speak	10 models	9 expert	9 students	9 entities
prototype	15 game	14 environment	13 politics	12 picture	11 general	11 trends	10 learning	9 embedded	9 linguistic	9 page
artifact	15 artifacts	14 clients	12 characteristics	12 scenario	11 self	11 solve	10 implementation	9 cognition	9 benefits	9 engagement
contextual	15 basic	13 user's	12 aspects	12 document	11 placement	11 rules	10 subtle	9 reflect	9 application	9 redesign
balance	15 details	13 personal	12 marketers	12 buttons	11 creativity	11 stage	10 feedback	9 purchase	9 phase	9 tech
awareness	15 map	13 connections	12 screen	12 tree	11 icons	11 integrity	10 opportunity	9 corporate	9 plan	9 metaphors
diagrams	15 sign	13 building	12 produced	12 honesty	11 intellectual	10 teams	10 practitioners	9 businesses	9 participants	9 affordances
disciplines	15 diagram	13 graphical	12 emphasis	12 material	11 requirements	10 issue	10 visually	9 bit	9 steps	8 power
tool	15 cultural	13 refined	12 society	12 spec	11 try	10 internet	10 message	9 errors	9 developers	8 styling
creations	14 consumer	13 production	12 competitive	11 gui	11 iterative	10 intuitive	10 feature	9 taught	9 gather	8 love
support	14 innovation	13 embrace	12 carnegie	11 perception	11 discovery	10 marketplace	10 writing	9 efficiency	9 navigation	8 china
qualities	14 services	13 rich	12 mellon	11 representation	11 review	10 device	10 logical	9 modern	9 humans	8 interact

A collection of reflections written
and compiled by Jon Kolko

Includes contributions from
Chris Connors
Justin Petro
Uday Gajendar
Ellen Beldner

THOUGHTS ON INTERACTION DESIGN

CONTENTS

This is a text intended to contemplate the theory behind the field of Interaction Design in a new way. There exist a number of texts that have already explored Interaction Design. Some of these consider the role of design in Human-Computer Interaction, a field bounded by Cognitive Psychology and Computer Science. These texts usually describe the nature of design as related to a user-interface design on a screen—emphasizing the specific elements that show up in an interface, or examining examples of best practices, heuristics, or guidelines for creating interfaces. This type of text is frequently found in schools of computer science and may actually be used as a textbook for engineering students interested in understanding the human-level repercussions of their actions.

Other texts explore the nature of design as related to the creation of two, three, or four dimensional forms. These texts look at aesthetic and emotional value provided by various shapes, compositions, or arrangements of elements. The mechanism for explaining formal choices is usually by example—showing a physical product, or demonstrating a particular interactive piece—illustrating the result of design work in a graphical way that emphasizes beauty and elegance. This type of text is often found in schools of design or fine arts and may be used to illustrate a historical precedence for a particular stylistic movement.

There are, however, few texts that explore the semantic connections that live between technology and form which are brought to life when someone uses a product. These connections may be thought of as "interactions" or "experiences", and are beginning to hint that a field known as Design (with a capitol "D") is a legitimately separate area of study alongside Science or Art. This text attempts to live in this area—to consider and reflect on the more theoretical and conceptual aspects of Interaction Design.

The author is fully aware that practicing Interaction Designers may find the contents of this text to be "high-level" or seemingly void of pragmatic or immediately applicable use. The purpose of this text is not to provide tools that can be applied in the role of day-to-day Interaction Design operations; other books do this quite well.

Instead, **it is the primary goal of this text to better define Interaction Design**: to provide a definition that encompasses the intellectual facets of the field, the conceptual underpinnings of Interaction Design as a legitimate human-centered field, and the particular methods used by practitioners in their day-to-day experiences. This definition and investigation centers around the issue of argument and rhetoric, and illustrates that Interaction Design is a form of communication that can be thought of as identical in nature to language. As Interaction Design is a vast subject, this text attempts to touch on many topics in a slight manner rather than one topic in a deep manner.

An additional goal of this text is to assure practicing Interaction Designers that they are not, in fact, simply tools to be used in the cleanup phases of a technology-centered project. Interaction Designers need to possess a great intellectual capacity for complicated problem solving, for dynamic inquiry relating to technology, and for substantial empathy of the human experience. This intellectual insight is ideal for solving strategic business problems and for humanizing technology, and the creation of "pretty interfaces" is perhaps the most blatant misuse of this critical resource.

A final goal of this text is to provide Interaction Designers with the vocabulary necessary to justify their existence to other team members: to engineers, to marketers, and ultimately, to management. Without this justification, these advocates for the humane manifestation of technology may end up as simple cogs in the wheel of technological progression.

Designers of all breeds bemoan their lack of representation in industry—they claim to be misunderstood, underpaid, and relegated to stylist or pixel pusher. If designers are, in fact, stylists, then they deserve to be paid to style: to create a temporary visual feeling that is transient and cheap. But Interaction Design is not about a transient aesthetic. A "cool flash interface" defines Interaction Design in the same way that accounting defines strategic business development—not at all. Interaction Designers are trained to observe humanity and to balance complicated ideas, and are used to thinking in opposites: large and small, conceptual and pragmatic, human and technical. They are the shapers of behavior. Behavior is a large idea, and may, at first blush, seem too large to warrant a single profession. But a profession has emerged nonetheless. This professional category includes the complexity of information architecture, the anthropologic desire to understand humanity, the altruistic nature of usability engineering, and the creation of dialogue.

While there is now a need for this profession in business—perhaps to truly *drive* business—the value of Interaction Design is not in the creation of profits; these are incidental. The value is, instead, in the development of human-centered designs and in the creation of a framework in which to experience these designs.

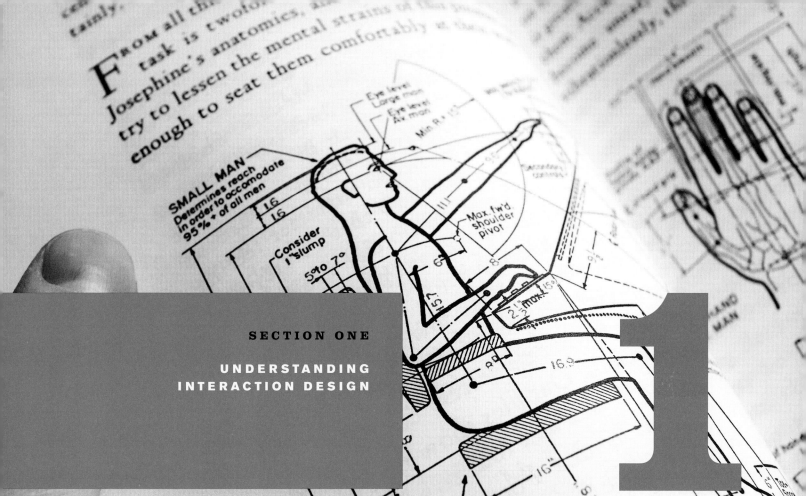

Interaction Design is the creation of a dialogue between a person and a product, service, or system. This dialogue is usually found in the world of behavior—the way someone may hold his knife and fork while cutting into a steak, or the way one chooses to purchase a beautiful chair, trading off cost for beauty or brand for convenience. Structuring dialogue is difficult, as it occurs in a fourth dimension—over time. To design behavior requires an understanding of the fluidity of natural dialogue, which is both reactionary and anticipatory at the same time. Common metrics for evaluating Interaction Design track the "ease of use" one has with negotiating an interface, yet usability is only a portion of a larger set of characteristics that become relevant during this dialogue. Objects, services and systems that have staying power frequently have qualities other than ease of use that cause them to become timeless, or priceless, or desirable.

These "other qualities" are subjective, and design has often been considered an applied art. Yet there is a subtle distinction between artist and designer. An artist makes a statement, a distinct argument, through his canvas or clay or metal, and the viewer responds. A conversation evolves, through acceptance, or rejection, or understanding, or bewilderment. The artist rarely claims a responsibility to the audience—many artists create because they like to, or because they feel that they "have to"—and clarity of message may be less relevant than a strong emotional reaction. "I do not understand your message, yet I understand that I do not like it." The audience is able to form opinions and actions without becoming intimate with the content.

The designer has a harder task. Design work is of function, and language, and meaning. Through visual and semantic language, a designer must create a design that assists the viewer not only in experiencing a particular emotion but also in truly understanding the content. This understanding goes deeper than just usability and is not isolated in a single instance in time. The audience must actually realize the intentions of the designer, and embrace the culture of the language that is presented. This language is not metaphorical. The designer does not design as language is spoken. In fact, design is language: the linguistic quality of form and content is indicated through context and use. The poet selects a topic and paints a vivid understanding of scene through character, time, and the beauty of the language. In a similar fashion, the product designer envisions an object and forms a vivid understanding of context through shape, weight, color, and material.

Interaction Designers, however, speak both words and form at once. They structure a compelling argument and invite the audience to share in their work. The work evolves over time, and the work is completed by the presence and synthesis of the audience. User-centered design, as frequently practiced, does not truly give credence to the importance of the "user." The creation lies dormant until the "user" honestly understands the beauty of what has been designed. If the user never understands this, then the creation is never actually "usable." This is not a noble and altruistic profession through intention, but rather through need.

Understanding the role of technology

Much praise has been written about the design of consumer electronics. Apple has been heralded by both business magazines and consumer reviews as the leader in innovation and authority on design; each new Motorola phone or Playstation release is announced as a huge leap forward in innovation. Yet these products—the best of the best—only hint at the capabilities of technology, if applied in a humanistic and aesthetically relevant manner. For at the end of the day, the music player is still a brick (albeit a much lighter brick than was previously available), and cell phones are still hard to use, and video games—while realistic—still follow the simple "kill it if it moves" gaming storylines of the early 1990s. These designs are not timeless, and they are not elegant. It is almost comical to wonder if these designs will be with us in five years, or in ten. Will people invite them into their houses for the rest of their lives, as they would a spouse? A more likely answer is that, in ten years, most consumers will have ditched their iPod for something younger and will have divorced the RAZR for something more beautiful.

Technology now affords a dramatic set of positive outcomes for humanity—massive social change, positively brilliant entertainment, and a more compelling understanding of self. The appropriate manifestation and use of technological advancements can bring about powerful change with regards to the mind, body, and soul. These benefits are made possible by advances in engineering, yet they will not be found by engineering advances alone. Nor will the benefits be realized by the business-savvy executives, as the problems are human problems first and business problems second. Instead, the changes will be realized by designers, and by a specific *breed* of designers: those creative designers who are both artists and engineers, and who are able to balance, over an extended period of time, technology and aesthetics without ever losing sight of the most important facet of design: humanity.

Interaction Design as a professional discipline

Interaction Design is recognized as a new field, but people have been designing interactions for centuries. The field has deeply embedded roots in various existing disciplines. As such, the subject frequently gets confused with some of these other fields, many of which share common names, acronyms, or techniques.

Interaction Design isn't necessarily the creation of websites. It isn't necessarily multimedia design, or graphical-user interface (GUI) design, and it doesn't even have to have a primary focus on *advanced* technology, although technology of *some* kind usually plays a significant role. A more appropriate, albeit academic definition of the field better reflects the working practitioner as well as predicts the future of this exciting profession: Interaction Design is the creation of a dialogue between a person and a product, system, or service. This dialogue is both physical and emotional in nature, and is manifested in form, function, and technology.

A simpler way of thinking about Interaction Designers is that they are the shapers of behavior. Interaction Designers—whether practicing as Usability Engineers, Visual Interface Designers, or Information Architects—all attempt to understand and shape human behavior. This is the purpose of the profession: to change the way people behave.

The field of Interaction Design has been acknowledged as a structured and unique discipline only in the past twenty years, generally in keeping with the pervasiveness and nature of technological change. As communication and computing technology has increased in speed, function, and capability, and decreased in size and cost, more and more consumer products can be found to contain some form of digitization. While this digital component frequently increases the overall utility of the product, it also serves to increase the complexity of the user experience. Thus, Interaction Designers find themselves performing usability evaluations on what were traditionally simple products, often in an attempt to ease the suffering of their end user. While Interaction Designers often work for the most financially motivated corporations, they frequently become the single champion for the consumer and spend a majority of their time trying to understand and model the "user's goals" as related to the business or technical goals.

Interaction Design borrows heavily from the field of psychology with regard to cognition, memory, and perception. It also draws equally from the world of art and design as it encompasses aesthetics and emotion. Successful Interaction Design affects a user on an emotional and highly personal level; a painting can be challenging, and so can an interactive product.

Interaction Design frequently gets confused with the design of websites, because people interact with websites and because web development teams find value in having Interaction Designers working with them. Interaction Design also gets mislabeled by business owners as *multimedia* or *interactive* design. While designers of interactive media certainly should be skilled in the techniques and methods described in this text, interactive media is almost always technologically centered rather than human centered. The majority of professional multimedia development is constrained to a specific software package and the capabilities associated with that, rather than centered around the constraints of an end user. For example, a recent job posting for a "Manager, Interactive Creative" position requires "Adobe Photoshop, Adobe ImageReady, Adobe Illustrator, Flash, HTML, DHTML. Ability to learn and adapt to new technologies and software. Familiar with Macromedia Dreamweaver, Flash and other similar programs. Understand and stay current with the capabilities of Internet-related technologies like: style-sheets, dynamic HTML, server-side programming, Javascript and Java." These are technologies, and while the person who ends up filling this position most likely understands the value of human-centered design, the job description implies a company culture that is strongly computing-centered. This tool-centeredness seems to indicate that a Design problem can be "fixed" by simply providing the right set of skills. In fact, the process of Design requires a rigorous methodology combined with this diverse set of skills and a tremendous amount of passion.

Designing and shaping behavior

Interaction Design is complicated. It is closely related to a number of important disciplines, and it encompasses many of these other fields. But the approach in the following pages attempts to reposition the field of Interaction Design away from a solely technical field or an artistic endeavor, and instead towards a duality that emphasizes the human side of technology. The Interaction Designer must become an expert in how human beings relate to each other, and to the world, and to the changing nature of technology and business. This understanding of behavior is important now in a *usability* sense, as technology has afforded the creation of massively complicated systems and services which people have a hard time comprehending. The understanding of behavior becomes more important—and hopefully a great deal more fun—when the potential of Interaction Design is realized: When Interaction Designers stop being advocates for simply usable designs and begin to herald the creation of more poetic design solutions.

Creations that transcend "usability" are those that resonate deeply and profoundly, and are those that make people *feel* passionately. We can consider a product as having attributes that are distinguishing character- istics, and these characteristics make us feel a certain way. The object becomes a vehicle for the designer to speak with a viewer, much like a painter uses a canvas to communicate with an audience.

One of the main distinctions between art and design, however, may be the bidirectional nature of the communication. Interaction Design is a dialogue. The designer speaks, and the user speaks back. Over time, the communication becomes involved. This may occur as a product becomes older and worn, or as a user becomes older and worn. Users change their innate responses to the object based on past experiences, perhaps through rote memorization or perhaps through a more associative integration of product into lifestyle. The ultimate goal of design, then, is to have a subtle, lasting and intuitive dialogue with a person, the same sort of dialogue a married couple may share after years together—the type of dialogue that occurs at a glance and often without a great deal of rational introspection. Implicit dialogue means an internal monologue that is com- municated through action. As we learn to "intuitively" use a product, we are in fact illustrating the scope of our past experiences with it. This is in direct opposition with "experience design." While we can mold activity through brute force or trial and error, Designers cannot create experiences with any degree of continuity. Instead, Interaction Designers exist to support experiences through the continual dialogue between people and products.

1

CHAPTER ONE:
MULTIPLE ROOTS, AND AN UNCERTAIN FUTURE

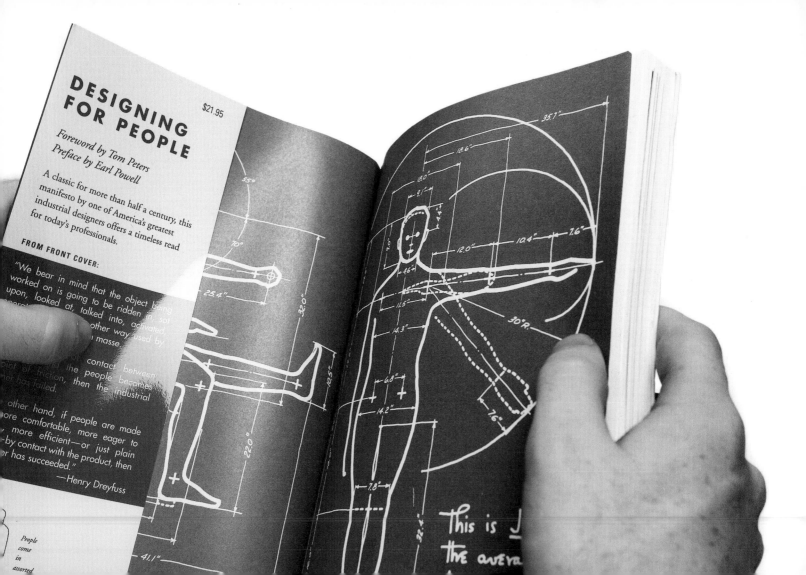

Interaction Designers find themselves in the unique position of being at the center of several worlds, all of which are presently colliding within the global marketplace. These worlds include industrial design, engineering, psychology, art, and business strategy. All of these elements must be present and well integrated in order to create a successful Interaction Design, and the Interaction Designer often seeks out the role of project manager—in charge of ensuring that all of these fields are adequately represented in the development of a product.

Human Factors in the creation of mass-produced objects

Interaction Designers must speak many languages, as they are facilitators between disciplines that have long since misunderstood each other or simply ignored one another's presence. One of these disciplines is Industrial Design, the field focused on the creation of mass-produced objects. This discipline finds its roots in the industrial revolution, as technology and manufacturing allowed for the creation of objects in multiples, and in a quick and cost-effective manner. Industrial Design is typically associated with the creation of furniture, appliances, and vehicles, and has been thought of as the profession responsible for the styling and aesthetic appeal of an object. This was certainly true at one point in time. Industrial Designers would be called in toward the end of the development of a product to "do the plastics" (essentially building a shell around the mass of gears, wires, and mechanisms inside of a complicated device). Industrial Designers often cringe, however, when introduced as the managers of form. For most practicing designers, Industrial Design is about much more than simple aesthetics or material choices. The professional world of product design and development has undergone a dramatic shift in

recent years as designers realized that they were not simply servants of style. *Real people* were using the products they were creating. This emphasis on people rather than on style was embodied in the subfield of Human Factors Engineering and was made popular in design by Henry Dreyfuss, the first president of the Industrial Design Society of America and a designer of everything from vacuums to locomotives. Dreyfuss found himself considering the physical dimensions, or anthropometry, of people in an effort to create both emotional and physical relationships between people and objects.[1]

This shift acknowledges a number of important considerations:
— people are unique, and have characteristics that may differ from the "average"
— designing for anthropometrics requires a different set of tools than designing for aesthetics
— the field of industrial design is larger than styling.

Dreyfuss published his pinnacle work in 1955, with the unintentionally ironic title *Designing for People* (who else would we be designing for?). This text included, among other things, the "austere line drawings of a man and a woman [who]… remind us that everything we design is used by people, and that people come in many sizes and have varying physical

---

1 Not surprisingly, this shift was brought about by the one major and consistent source of cultural change found throughout history: war. Designers working on various projects for the United States Army during World War II were required to create equipment relevant for the large quantity of differently shaped soldiers. Aircraft cockpits were notoriously uncomfortable and hard to use, and after enough pilots experienced "failure" (and crashed their planes), the Army began incorporating psychologists and human-centered engineers into their development process.

attributes."[2] These line drawings of Joe and Josephine brought the first glimpse of a truly human perspective to the design of mass-produced products, as they included the precise measurements of the human figure (from very small to very large). What a subtle and important shift in the creation of goods—to consider who would use them once they were created! This ultimately became quantified as a profession known as Human Factors, and was further expanded in the late 1980s, as Industrial Designers began to acknowledge both issues of physical stature as well as constraints related to perception, cognition, and memory. The growing mechanical and electrical complexity of mass-produced objects increased the potential for cognitive friction, and designers increasingly struggled to understand the limitations the human body places on the development of products. An interesting relationship was established between Human Factors Engineers and Industrial Designers. While the two disciplines were obviously and closely related, the scientific grounding of Human Factors research led towards a more refined, academic, and respected profession. The PhD is presently considered the terminal degree in studies of Human Factors, and many who obtain the doctorate and return to industry go on to work at corporations producing large and highly complicated physical and digital creations (such as airplanes). Design, however, continually gets relegated to the status of an applied art—the MFA, a degree in Fine Arts, is considered by many to be the terminal degree in Industrial Design. Thus, while there are many designers who both understand and respect the importance of physical, perceptual, and cognitive human factors, there are a great many who were never formally instructed in the relationships

between these fields. Advances in technology, advances in materials, and a general love of form frequently take precedence over consideration of the human use of both physical and digital products. Usability is still discussed in business as a competitive differentiator—as an "extra" that can help distinguish products in the marketplace. Consider the number of times a physical or digital product has caused a high degree of frustration: When a user finds it difficult to turn the English subtitles off while viewing an American DVD, or when he can't set the clock on a brand new car, the user has experienced the results of a prioritization of some other element over the human element. This may be technology, or aesthetics, or cost—but something has been given more importance than "designing for people," with people left to bear the brunt of that decision.

Industrial Designers continue to create objects of desire, balancing formal qualities with human-centered constraints in both major corporations and in design consultancies such as Fitch or Ziba. There is a continued realization, however, that the creation of mass-produced objects in the United States may be nearing its demise. The Chinese have nearly taken over production of manufactured goods, to the point where it is cost effective for even the Taiwanese to outsource their creations to mainland China.[3] The hundreds of design schools in China are producing thousands of capable, eager, and—most important—cheap designers. Chinese designers and engineers can soon offer the entire package of product development skills necessary to bring products to market, and at a substantial discount as compared to their American counterparts. The field of Industrial Design is threatened in the United States, and many

2 Dreyfuss, Henry. Reprinted by Permission. *Designing for People*. Allworth Press, 2003. p26.

3 Huang, Chung-Yi. *Taiwan's Design Identity*. Thesis, Savannah College of Art and Design, Savannah, Georgia, USA. 2005. p6.

designers are beginning to wonder if there are any core Industrial Design skills that *cannot* be outsourced. What jobs will remain for those designers who wish to stay in America?

Design strategist Elaine Ann explores this very issue in a short but poignant article entitled "The Top 10 Myths and Truths about Design in China." As she explains, not all product development *is* going to China: "DESIGN is a very big word, from designing a corporate brand strategy, designing an innovative way of cleaning, or designing the styling of a toothbrush—we all call it 'design.' The bad news is if you are in the last category of 'design' — product form-making or styling business — it is very likely that such design services will truly move to China… Designers in the U.S. need to quickly engage in more strategic levels of design, and to create innovations that revolutionize businesses." [4]

Human Factors in the creation of software

As the shift from pure aesthetics towards human factors was occurring in Industrial Design, an interesting and, in hindsight, nearly identical shift was occurring within the development of software products. Software engineers had typically created software to suit the functionality required by the business or that was afforded by the technology. The fact that a person was required to interact with a software solution was frequently ignored, as the presence of computing technology alone was often remarkable enough to sell products. *Software design* was unheard of, and if a "designer" was included in the process at all, it might have been in the capacity of a stylist—to make the ANSI graphics a bit more appealing

4 Elaine Ann, Kaizor Innovation. Founder/Director.
<http://www.core77.com/reactor/08.04_china.asp>

to the eye. A great deal of the software that existed in the early 80s was not "designed" at all; instead, it was simply engineered. As computer systems began to grow in size and scope, however, a subset of computer engineering was created to deal with the complexity as it was made more apparent to the user. This world of Usability Engineering sought to make computers more usable. "User friendly," now considered by both Designers and Usability Engineers alike to be cliché and simplistic, was a fair goal to keep in mind; the norm was decidedly unfriendly, as computers continually reported "fatal errors" (or, in the case of the original Apple Macintosh, a small icon of a bomb being displayed when trouble arose).

Usability Engineers primarily worked on the large mainframes or back-office computer systems of big corporations like Nynex or Xerox or IBM. This work was inherently tied to principles of cognitive psychology, as these engineers needed to understand the stresses memory could handle and where perception and cognition failed. *Usability Inspection Methods*, a landmark text on assessing the usability of complicated computer systems, was originally published in 1994 and included methodologies like the heuristic evaluation method, pluralistic walkthrough method, and cognitive walkthrough method. These names reflect the nature of much of the usability work being done in the late 1980s and early 1990s: Highly complicated systems were confusing, difficult to use, and boring, and the Usability Engineers attempted to fix at least the first two points. The low-hanging fruit was usability. By making the systems easier to use, a majority of the cognitive friction would disappear and business could reap the potential profits. Jakob Nielsen, then an engineer at SunSoft (of Sun Microsystems), developed several guidelines for the creation of usable software. One of the guidelines present in Nielsen's widely cited and taught Heuristic Evaluation methodology is "Aesthetic and minimalist design: Dialogues should not contain information which is irrelevant or rarely needed. Every extra unit of information in a dialogue competes with the relevant units of information and diminishes their relative usability."[5] The guideline advocates for simplicity: remove extra aesthetic elements, as they compete with efficiency, time on task, or number of errors.

Usability engineering is not new—at least not when considered in the guise of the computing revolution and modern, desktop computers. Finding usability-centered articles in popular magazines and in newspapers, however, is a more recent phenomenon. The presence of vocabulary and content relating to usability testing in more approachable texts (like *Business Week*, *The Wall Street Journal*, or *The New York Times*) may be due to the explosion in popularity of the Internet and the World Wide Web in the past decade. The complexity of the relationships between websites, hardware and software is such that audiences have begun to understand—and demand—more from their products.

The implications of this popularity, however, are both good and bad. On the one hand, usability practitioners are being pushed to reduce complexity and unnecessary difficulties in products, and the outcome of these activities includes the creation of solutions that are easier to use and to understand. However, the presence of the usability-centered vocabulary in popular culture, such as with the design of web sites, has created a misconception as to the fields of usability engineering, usability testing, and Interaction Design. There now exists an overwhelming number of people who fancy themselves "web designers"—skilled at the creation of simple web sites, but not in the rich and intellectual underpinnings of

Usability or Design proper. Interaction Designers find themselves in the awkward position of trying to explain that "Why yes, I do work on web sites, but that's just a tiny portion of my job." Richard Buchanan, former head of the School of Design at Carnegie Mellon University, discusses the humanization of technical fields without resorting to subjugation: "Design is not a trivial aspect of the development of information technologies; it is the central discipline for humanizing all technologies, turning them to human purpose and enjoyment."[6]

At the heart of the "usability engineering" phenomenon is an understanding of the humans who are experiencing a product—understanding how their brain works, how their memory works, and how they make complicated decisions in order to complete tasks and achieve goals. This understanding can be grounded formally in the fields of perceptual and cognitive psychology. Understanding limits to comprehension becomes of critical importance when tasks become complicated. Frequently, human factors engineers work to develop complicated systems, such as air traffic control interfaces or controls for planes—generally, demanding tasks that require snap decisions based on a great deal of immediately appearing data. It may not be appropriate for one trained in the visual arts (i.e., one trained to trust his intuition) to "intuit" the layout of a control panel on a Boeing 777. The potential for catastrophic error seemingly outweighs the need for aesthetically pleasing interfaces.

Usability Engineering—and the aforementioned Jakob Nielsen himself—became in vogue in popular culture as business embraced the World Wide Web as another distribution channel for products and struggled to

---

5 Nielsen, Jakob. "Heuristic Evaluation." *Usability Inspection Methods*. Ed Jakob Nielsen and Robert L Mack. Wiley, 1994.

6 Buchanan, Richard. "Good Design in the Digital Age." *GAIN: AIGA Journal of Design for the Network Economy*. Vol 1, No 1. October, 2000.

understand how it could best utilize this new medium to its financial advantage. Nielsen has had a great deal of success marketing guidelines for web usability, with articles entitled "21 guidelines for making Flash easier to use for users with disabilities" and "65 guidelines for serving individual and institutional investors, financial analysts, and business journalists on corporate websites."[7] While these articles provide very concrete and alluring recommendations for usability improvements, they simultaneously diminish the importance of the other aspects of experience. Emphasis is placed on following guidelines rather than examining real people. While a major facet of Interaction Design is grounded in Usability Engineering (and therefore deeply embedded in computer science), the discipline is quickly growing much larger—and more robust—than can be contained in a set of guidelines or principles.

Usability engineering as a form of applied psychology is utilitarian and can even be thought of as altruistic. Psychology has crept into the development of products in a more sinister way as well. Ralph Caplan recalls that "In the 1950s Freudian market researchers invaded product design, led by psychoanalyst Dr. Ernest Dichter, who found that in the buried fantasies of the male consumer, a convertible really meant a mistress,

while a sedan symbolized wife and family."[8] Attempts to psychoanalyze consumers have grown in the development of recent products, and the role of marketer seems to have shifted from announcing "what *we have*" to illustrating "what *you could have,*" and finally, to trying to force a consumer to realize "what *you think you need.*"

For the most part, however, cognitive psychologists involved in Interaction Design activities attempt to reconcile the limits of human behavior with the advances of technology, and to utilize technology in a way to help the human condition. Ken Koedinger, a professor at Carnegie Mellon University, creates cognitive models—computer simulations of thinking and learning, which are then used to develop educational materials and programs. These models have been used successfully in the development of tutoring software that appropriately responds to an individual's methods of

7 The Internet finds many critiques of this very analytical approach to web usability. Frank Spillers, a web and usability expert, says, "One of the things I have noticed about people who take Nielsen's teachings at face value is that they end up communicating like him. The blaming, critical and self-righteous tones that characterize Nielsen's articles and interviews are not to be confused with how a professional usability consultant ought to communicate. Of the hundreds of people I have trained in the past few years, I have noticed the 'Critical Jakob' in their findings. The danger is that armed with Jakob's influence, we can assume that we have a hammer large enough to break anything."

8 Caplan, Ralph. *By Design: Why There Are No Locks on the Bathroom Doors in the Hotel Louis XIV and Other Object Lessons.* Fairchild Books & Visuals, 2005. p231.

problem solving. In fact, Koedinger explains that this type of program—for example, an Algebra Cognitive Tutor—has helped students outperform their peers by as much as 100% on real world problem solving.[9]

Convergent product design creates new challenges

The parallel growth of Industrial Design focusing on the human body, and usability engineering and cognitive psychology focusing on the human mind, can in hindsight be thought of as the roots of the convergent product design solutions we are beginning to enjoy today. As these two worlds begin to collide due primarily to the miniaturization of technology and the ease—and cost—of integrating digital components into physical devices, a new breed of designer has been given the difficult task of creating convergent products that are actually easy to use and pleasant to encounter. And just in time, as the roots of both physical and digital product development seem to be turning quickly into "commodity" fields, where quality and function are nearly ubiquitous and cost becomes the only differentiator in service. As software development is unloaded to India, and physical product development makes its way to China, the cohesion of user experience across physical and digital creations becomes both critical and highly difficult.

This split also begs the question: If the technology is going to India, and the form is going to China, what is left for the United States? The answer is Interaction Design, in a rich manifestation of mind, body, and soul. One of the more strategic levels of design encompasses Interaction Design as defined in this text: the creation of a meaningful relationship between a product and a person, identified and created through ethnographic and other user-centered design methods. Interaction Design is positioned to become a strategic differentiator for businesses looking for innovative differentiation, and thus the field is a likely evolution for many Industrial Designers. This strategic level of design is one that Interaction Design is prepared to participate in, and even own—if this type of designer is able to speak the common language of business and strategy. A great number of analysts have predicted just this sort of respect and strategic placement of design within traditional businesses. Daniel Pink, an author and business strategist, has been quoted repeatedly in major news publications as saying that "The MFA is becoming the new MBA."[10]

The buzz surrounding this simple meme illustrates a glimmer of hope for businesses pushing and retaining creativity within the standard business development process.

9 Koedinger recalls an example of the early effects his advanced technology had on self-declared technophobes (high school teachers). The team of software developers received a phone call from a high school teacher. The teacher was livid, demanding to know why the tutor was swearing at students. Astounded, Koedinger's team analyzed line after line of the program, trying to find what rogue code could possibly be the culprit. When the developers found nothing wrong in the code, they asked the teacher to print the screen of the tutor the next time this happened. Sure enough, a few days later the teacher was on the phone again, triumphantly stating that they had evidence that the tutor was mistreating the students and calling them dumb. Sure enough, there it was in black and white: "I do not understand why you are such a dumbass." Koedinger quickly realized that a savvy student had determined the way the tutor responded to invalid input: "I do not understand *(repeat unknown command).*" The student entered "why you are such a dumbass," and the computer responded appropriately: "I do not understand **why you are such a dumbass.**" And then the student, proud as punch, called the teacher over and said, "See! It's doing it again!" Artificial intelligence, indeed.

10 Pink, Daniel. *A Whole New Mind.* Riverhead, 2005. p74.

Pink goes on to explain that "businesses are realizing that the only way to differentiate their goods and services in today's overstocked, materially abundant marketplace is to make their offerings transcendent—physically beautiful and emotionally compelling."[11] Traditionally, however, those who understand and embrace creativity seem to have a strong aversion to business (the opposite is also true). Art school brings to mind images of pierced parts and colorful hair, and doesn't usually elicit thoughts of the stoic, walnut-trimmed board room. Creativity alone is not enough. This creative force needs to be managed, understood, and strategically applied. This management can only be attained by one who can bridge the gap between the "suits" and the "freaks." This is one with strong creative thinking skills, vocabulary relating to business and strategy, and the ability to blend easily into a diverse set of cultures. The historic intermingling of Industrial Design, Psychology, and Business Development points towards a future of mass-produced, innovative products that function "under the radar" of our cognition—products that are usable, useful, and desirable. Interaction Design is the discipline best prepared to take on the project management associated with the development of these products, as Interaction Designers are formally trained in understanding culture, managing creativity, and forging relationships between multiple disciplines.

11 Ibid.

CHAPTER TWO:
COMPUTING AND HUMAN COMPUTER INTERACTION

Computers were not intended to be vehicles for entertainment and content delivery. Computers were intended to compute. Highly specialized work required highly specialized machinery, and the computational ability of the machine that used vacuum tubes and punched cards was not thought to be of much use for anyone outside of a small circle of like-minded engineers. That circle, however, contained a number of great thinkers, scientists and generals: the military can be credited for advancing, from idea to production, many of the technical advances we take for granted today.

Understanding the history of human-computer interaction

The specialized nature of individual computational projects identified early computers, such as the UNIVAC in 1951 (which was originally intended to assist the United States government in completing the census) or the ENIAC I in 1946 (which was supported by the military to assist their development of artillery-firing tables). These computers were good at performing simple and discrete tasks, and were custom solutions to custom problems. A subtle shift occurred in 1952, however, when IBM announced the development of the 701:

> "Our progress in electronics convinced us one year ago that we had in our company the ability to create for the Defense Department, and the defense industries, a computer of advanced design which could be of major service to our national defense effort.… We began planning and building such a machine, which we believe will be the most advanced, most flexible high-speed computer in the world. It is built not for one special purpose but as a general purpose device, and two days after it was announced on a limited confidential basis we had orders for ten… The new calculator takes less than one-quarter the space of the previous machine. It is difficult to compare speeds, but we feel conservatively that the new calculator is 25 times faster than our old one and far more flexible. In addition, the new machine is a commercial machine which will be rented and serviced with our regular line of products."[12] [Emphasis added.]

While still seemingly driven by a patriotic sense of duty, International Business Machines clearly had a more commercial motive, and this can be considered the launch of computing as a business tool—a tool intended for increased productivity across business tasks, and, ultimately, increased revenue. After the successful launch of the 701, IBM commenced with the rapid development of additional high end, room sized, expensive business machines. The machines got faster and smaller, and were viewed in business circles as the tools of automation necessary to make the enterprise run smoother and leaner. This remained true until a significant event occurred in 1968. This event was relatively unknown outside of computing culture, but it was an event that has so obviously shaped the heart of the information age.

----

12   It is interesting to note that, even in 1946, the general notion of Moore's law is present (the computational speed will increase exponentially over time) and the heralding of "faster and smaller" is being used to sell technology.
<http://www-03.ibm.com/ibm/history/exhibits/701/701_announced.html>, courtesy of IBM Corporate Archives.

In 1968, in the Convention Center in San Francisco, a group of over a thousand hackers[13] listened and watched as a handsome young man quietly sat beneath an enormous display. The man had a soft, hypnotizing voice, and for nearly 90 minutes, he held the room of engineers captivated as he demonstrated one miraculous vision after another. At this conference, Doug Engelbart, a researcher at the Augmentation Research Center (ARC) at the Stanford Research Institute (SRI) in Menlo Park, California, presented a working system that highlighted—for the very first time, ever—windowed displays, a graphical user interface, networking, hyperlinks, audio and video "conferencing," dynamic file linking, shared-screen collaboration and a mouse. "It is almost shocking to realize that in 1968 it was a novel experience to see someone use a computer to put words on a screen... Those who were in the audience at Civic Auditorium that afternoon remember how Doug's quiet voice managed to gently but irresistibly seize the attention of several thousand high-level hackers for nearly two hours, after which the audience did something rare in that particularly competitive and critical subculture—they gave Doug and his colleagues a standing ovation." [14]

Engelbart publicly outlined a vision of computing as a truly human-centered tool, a tool that can be used to achieve great feats for the individual. While his work would not be found in a commercially available form until some years later, this little known event in 1968 can truly be thought of as the beginning of the "information age."

The impact of Doug Engelbart's vision of computing may not have been realized immediately, yet his vision spread quietly as a number of his friends and students began to find their way into the worlds of academic research. Xerox PARC was the next major contributor to the world of computing and included a number of Doug's disciples. Xerox PARC can be thought of as the first workspace that formally embraced Interaction Designers. Xerox Corporation's mission for PARC, when it was officially founded in July of 1970, was to create "the architecture of information."[15] By 1973, the Xerox Alto was commercially available, and eleven years before the original Macintosh computer was released in 1984 the Alto included a What-You-See-Is-What-You-Get (WYSIWYG) editor, a mouse, a graphical user interface (GUI), bit-mapped display, menus, icons, windows, and Ethernet: the ability to communicate to a larger network.

But even PARC missed the beauty of its creation. The engineers at PARC failed to see that the computer could be used for something outside of the worlds of efficiency or productivity. The idea of *one man, one computer* was novel and unique, but did not transcend the then-established notion of a computer as a business tool—a fairly benign object intended to make transactions faster. It took a particularly savvy individual

---

13 Brian Harvey, a Professor of Computer Science at Berkeley, explains that a computer hacker "... is someone who lives and breathes computers, who knows all about computers, who can get a computer to do anything. Equally important, though, is the hacker's attitude. Computer programming must be a hobby, something done for fun, not out of a sense of duty or for the money." <http://www.cs.berkeley.edu/~bh/hacker.html>

14 Rheingold, Howard. *Tools for Thought: The History and Future of Mind-Expanding Technology.* MIT Press, 2000. p188. Also available online: <http://www.rheingold.com/texts/tft/9.html>

15 PARC History. <http://www.parc.com/about/history/default.html>

to grasp the potential for a *human* use of technology: Steve Jobs.[16] As Jobs toured PARC, he saw the future of computing. "And they showed me really three things. But I was so blinded by the first one I didn't even really see the other two. One of the things they showed me was object orienting programming… the other one they showed me was a networked computer system… they had over a hundred Alto computers all networked using email etc., etc. I didn't even see that. I was so blinded by the first thing they showed me which was the graphical user interface. I thought it was the best thing I'd ever seen in my life… within, you know, ten minutes it was obvious to me that all computers would work like this some day."[17]

Many digital designers consider Engelbart's work, and the extended development that followed at PARC, to be the birth of a new field of computing dedicated to the ambiguous "art" of crafting how people relate to machines. HCI, or Human Computer Interaction, has become the name for this field, and can be formally defined as the "discipline concerned with the design, evaluation and implementation of interactive computing systems for human use and with the study of major phenomena surrounding them."[18] After PARC was created, one can see how the momentum of human-centered computing built and built over two decades until the Macintosh was released in 1984. The Macintosh indicated a dramatic shift from the notion of computing as *specialized* work (computational) to computing as used in *all* work, and finally to computing used *in the home*. This path extends the field of HCI from dealing with primarily the implementation of computing systems toward the understanding of how people "interface" with technology.

In the field of HCI, a particular style of interface design quickly arose as the norm. This interface system included windows, icons, menus, and pointing (and clicking), and became known as WIMP. The interface style was found in the original Alto, in Apple's first major graphical user interface-driven computer the LISA, and also in the Apple Macintosh. WIMP has lived far longer than was ever expected, as it is the same paradigm found in modern-day Macintosh and Windows operating systems. Jef Raskin, one of the original designers credited with the Apple Macintosh operating system, was working diligently to develop an alternative to WIMP prior to his death in 2005. "The Mac is now a mess… One only cares about getting something done. Apple has forgotten this key concept."[19] While WIMP was once novel and unique, it appeared that Raskin became frustrated with the emphasis on aesthetics or graphics at the expense of usability.

With the development of WIMP came the general notion that computers could and should be used by the masses. The text-input command line was certainly enough to turn off non-technical individuals, and the direct-manipulation of overlapping windows—along with clever marketing

16 Jobs did not, as it is commonly considered, "steal" the idea of a graphical user interface from Xerox. In fact, Apple negotiated a stock-for-visit trade with Xerox, and implicit in the visitation was the rights to use a number of the ideas that the visitors viewed as they toured PARC. It has been argued that Jobs is not a savvy businessman and that his success at Apple has been a fluke; this seems to indicate the contrary, and might be the business deal of the century.

17 PBS: Triumph of the Nerds, Program Transcription.
<http://www.pbs.org/nerds/part3.html> Text provided courtesy of Oregon Public Broadcasting.

18 Card, Stu, et al. *Curricula for Human-Computer Interaction*. ACM SIGCHI, 1992/1996.
<http://sigchi.org/cdg/cdg2.html#2_1> Association for Computing Machinery, Inc. Reprinted by permission.

19 Walsh, Jason. "Talk time: Jef Raskin." *The Guardian*. October 21, 2004.
<http://technology.guardian.co.uk/online/story/0,3605,1331536,00.html>

from Apple—made the machine more accessible to most families. Much has been written about the two decades following the release of the Apple Macintosh computer, usually with an emphasis on the increasing capabilities of computers and the exponential growth both Apple and Microsoft enjoyed. While the majority of the historical texts attempts to understand the changes that occurred in the field of computers and computing, a broader look at the improvements of technology-driven products identifies an interesting growth of computer-like products that are called other things. Cellular phones, digital cameras, and other consumer electronics are, in fact, computers with different physical manifestations. Many practitioners in the field of HCI are beginning to consider the pragmatic implications technological advancement has on their profession. What if the "computer" as commonly understood is changed to another form—a form with different sizes and constraints, or a form without a screen?

Cyborgs and the ubiquity of technology

The work of Steve Mann, formerly of MIT, illustrates one view of the technology-driven "computerless" future: Mann has dedicated over twenty years to investigating the nature of a *cyborg,* the science fiction driven vision of a half man, half machine. Mann refers to himself as Cyberman and wears a heads-up display embedded in his sunglasses. He also carries a hip-pack-style computer, which enables him to record and recall video, imagery, and other data during a casual conversation.[20] The following Mann has created is impressive, with a number of students at both MIT

20 McMullan, Erin. "Cyberman (2001)." *Idea Idee: Digitaleve Canada's Webzine.*
<http://wearcam.org/cyberman_antithetical_relationship_of_art_mathematics_
physics_technology.htm>

and the University of Toronto running around campus with dark glasses and wires streaming about their bodies. While the students are able to play a real-life version of the Matrix, these same young technologists have the very genius necessary to go on to manage the companies that are increasingly present in our lives. Microsoft, a particularly technologically-centered company, envisions a Connected Home—the lights turn on when you enter, and your thermostat adjusts to your particular preferences. This technology-centered view of the future that can be seen in the science fiction movies is decidedly unfamiliar. Practitioners involved in HCI struggle to make these cyborg-inspired tools easier to use, and struggle equally as hard to illustrate the implications of a "blue screen of death" on a thermostat. Underlying the development of these technologies seems to be a highly rhetorical but critically important question: Do people *want* these things in their house? Technology is the driving force behind these innovations, and humanity is left to cope as best as possible when these technical "advancements" reach the marketplace.

Recently, there has been a great deal of attention and effort placed on the creation of this type of smart device or applied computing. Academics and industry practitioners alike are investigating ways to embed computing in various locations around the home or even on the body. Many of these investigations are driven by engineering innovations, and while technically quite impressive, few engineers or product managers seem to be asking the difficult question of "why?" Why produce a refrigerator that knows when it is out of milk? Why create lighting systems that turn themselves on or off when a person enters or leaves the room? Those engaged in HCI activities—Interaction Designers—exist to ask these difficult questions, and to create frameworks for compelling experiences rather than technical experiences. Interaction Design has outgrown its computing roots, and is now a field responsible for humanizing technology.

The history of Interaction Design, then, is painted by a constant and rapid growth of technology and then a struggle to make that technology behave. The past twenty years show HCI professionals engaging in Usability Engineering, and Human Factors Engineers working with Industrial Designers to tame the complexity created by technological advancements. Deeply entrenched in companies and organizations are individuals who are advocating for humanity, rather than for technology. These individuals are slowly finding ways to transition toward the creation of designs that are not simply usable but are useful and desirable as well.

INTERACTION DESIGN IN AN ENGINEERING-CENTRIC WORLD

Chris Connors, Apple

Chris Connors is currently employed at Apple. Prior to working at Apple, Chris worked at NASA with a focus on designing future mission support tools for planning robotic activity during surface operations on Mars. Chris also has an extensive background with Trilogy Software in Austin, Texas, where he designed enterprise software products for the Financial Services, Telecommunications, Computer, and Automotive industries. Chris was one of two lead designers for Trilogy subsidiary carOrder.com, winner of PC Magazine's Editor's Choice Award for Best Online Car Buying site in 1999.

It's hard to believe that a decade has elapsed since Carnegie Mellon University, having reputable Design, Computer Science, and Cognitive Psychology programs, decided to offer a graduate degree program focused on a discipline coalescing at the intersection of the three. When I entered the marketplace as a newly conferred graduate with a Masters in Human Computer Interaction, I can recall trying to explain to my family and friends exactly what HCI was—something I still occasionally find myself doing. Describing our discipline to potential employers was a recurring challenge: Many were confused by a CS degree without production programming, a design degree that didn't deal primarily with product form, or a cognitive psychologist who wasn't solely focused on modeling human performance or conducting experimentally-driven usability testing.

Today's employment prospects are dramatically different. Each week, BayCHI distributes nearly 80 job listings seeking precisely the sort of multidisciplinary candidates the HCI Masters program at Carnegie

Mellon University continues to produce (albeit in greater quantities) to this day—and that's only jobs in the Bay area. In my own recent experience on both sides of the job market I found hiring managers eager for competent Interaction Designers; engineers desperate for design resources to provide direction and structure, and other Interaction Designers seeking capable colleagues. Yet there are still plenty of companies in software, hardware, and aerospace that focus on engineering first and human factors second, with Interaction Design rarely ranking at all. How can Interaction Designers best integrate design process into these of organizations? Consider this trio of strategies, which have positioned teams in these types of organizations for success:

— Defining and employing a design process as a mechanism to set, manage, and fulfill expectations.
— Establishing and maintaining the design team's credibility with implementers, stakeholders, and users.
— Judiciously using prototypes of varying and often mixed fidelity to convey design intent, collect data, and create enthusiasm for your ideas.

In this discussion we'll hope to illuminate in practice how these methods can really enhance the relationships and output of integrated engineering and design teams.

Process

It's hard to imagine any design training that doesn't include process as a significant part of the studio experience. Put simply, process drives repeatability—reducing the reliance on inspiration—and creates a framework in which creative professionals can execute. Developers and engineers are also familiar with the use of process as a framework in which to increase the odds of repeatable results, and most have training and experience using a variety of software development processes. However, most have little experience with the **Understand** | **Design** | **Validate** | **Deliver** sorts of processes frequently applied in design disciplines. Their own experience using a variety of engineering processes creates common ground for the two disciplines, and creates opportunities for setting expectations between the disciplines.

The first step is, of course, to select a design process, adopt it, and use it. Most designers are used to employing a design process, most likely the one employed by their source of design or studio training. Without proposing one over another, the suggestion here is to get the design team to adopt and standardize a single process, define the range and types of deliverables for each process phase, and then, consistently apply it. By achieving consensus on process, phases, and deliverables, engineers, program managers, and stakeholders can develop consistent expectations about what sort of things they'll receive when regardless of the design resource assigned to their project.

Invest resources in educating engineers and management about your process. Many professionals outside the design discipline find the creative process to be mysterious and opaque with almost no expectations around the sort of output and deliverables they might expect from the process, save a design spec at the conclusion. Educating engineers about what sorts of activities and deliverables are part of the Understanding phase, for example, sets their expectations so that when your designers meet engineers and stakeholders to review competitive analyses and site flows diagrams, they won't immediately be frustrated at another meeting without a design spec. By clearly indicating what deliverables they can expect when, designers can manage and meet expectations within the groups.

In the design process, it's not uncommon to have to return to previous phases. Particularly in environments where clients or executives have the vision themselves to recognize that designers are not on a path to success, it's not uncommon to return to gather broader understanding about a domain, or competitors, or influences, for example. When design is linked to a delivery schedule, however, project managers and engineers can be uncomfortable with what they perceive as "starting over." However, similar events can occur for engineers or developers. It's not uncommon to find a method or algorithm that initially seemed viable in practice might not scale adequately, or offer the required performance, causing engineers to have to re-think their approach. Should designers find themselves in a state where they need to re-assess assumptions, use this common ground to build rapport, assess schedule impact, and move on.

As designers are proposing the schedule of activities as they move through their design process, be flexible about the duration of each activity. It might be difficult to gain broad understanding of a complex domain in only a few days, but the schedules may only allow that amount of time. Rather than fight for more time, design teams are better off executing under the schedule constraints, with the caveat that there's additional uncertainty (and likelihood of a revisiting design direction). It's important to pick your battles—fight for the things that are important (like getting ahead of the development cycle) and acquiesce the things that aren't (where you physically sit relative to the other designers or developers).

It's also important to recognize that just as there are numerous design processes out there, so too are there a variety of software development processes. While the relationship between design and traditional development styles such as Waterfall is pretty well established, the growing popularity of "agile" development methods offers an entirely new set of rules, and a real opportunity for education and evangelism.

"Agile" development methods, such as extreme Programming ("XP") and Scrum, are intended to give developers the flexibility to respond dynamically to changing requirements. However, the iterative process of designing the implementation shouldn't be mistaken for the iterative process of designing the product. What agile methods offer designers are an opportunity to design the product in a broad sense, and then the chance to execute designs in manageable sections over the development cycle. Designers may have to do some selling in order to convince developers to afford them some time up front to get ahead of the development cycle, but it's proven incredibly valuable to the HCI Group at NASA's Ames Research Center, as they've worked with the development teams at both their own center and at Jet Propulsion Laboratories in Pasadena, California. The team was approached about collaborating with developers working on the next generation of software tools for managing robotic surface operations on Mars, and the three teams have worked diligently and successfully striking a balance between the demands of XP, integrating design process, and managing remote developers for more than 3 years.

The HCI Group began by defining a framework under which the suite of tools would be developed, defining broad design direction for the application using wireframes, design documents, and even a dynamic wiki environment linked directly into the developers' bug tracking tool. The framework was vetted and validated with stakeholders and users, and set the development effort on a path towards success. Designers would then work a few weeks ahead of the developers, exploring functionality, testing designs, and developing specifications for sections of functionality ("search data," for example). The results of this effort have been enthusiastically received by their users, and are scheduled for use on two upcoming Mars missions.

Credibility

Once a design team has codified their process, educated engineers and stakeholders about the outputs and timing of their delivery, and executed as they've promised, one of the beneficial consequences should be growing credibility throughout the organization. Setting reasonable expectations and achieving them is one of the single most important things a design team can accomplish in terms of establishing a good baseline of credibility, but it's not the only thing.

A designer can gain a tremendous amount of knowledge and respect from stakeholders and users through the embedding process, as possible. For example, if an online retailer wants their designers to better understand and espouse the same "voice" employed at their brick-and-mortar locations, what better way than to train a designer and staff him at a retail location for a week or two? If a designer wants to understand the service gaps his application leaves between his customers and their goals, staffing him to participate as phone support is an excellent way to help him feel the user's pain.

The Ames HCI Group has enjoyed good results using this strategy. In 2003, having collaborated successfully with researchers on planning tools for the Mars exploration Rovers, designers were trained and embedded to support mission scientists utilizing planning tools. Staffed as both support personnel for Tactical Activity Planning and as researchers observing the process of collaborative scientific discovery, team members had almost unfettered access to the mission participants and their tools.

Tactical Activity Planning occurred nightly during the first 90 "sols"—or Martian solar days—of the mission (the "nominal" mission). Since each rover was expected to last only 90 sols before succumbing to the buildup of Martian dust (which would gradually block the solar panels until they could no longer recharge the spacecraft's batteries), every minute of Martian daylight was precious. Martian sols are 37 minutes longer than Earth days, and, in order to maximize robotic activity during those precious 90 sols, the mission was run on "Martian time"; researchers synched their respective clocks and watches with the Martian time. This meant the researchers were moving forward 40 minutes each day—the meeting scheduled for 8 am local time the first day would be at 8:40 am local time the next day, until it was occurring at around 8 *pm* local time 18 sols later.

While even the slightly romanticized JPL robot mascots gave web visitors the impression that the robots used onboard autonomous planning to sort out its daily activities, the reality was that mission planners kept the robots on a pretty tight leash, handing in carefully formed plans generated each night to dictate activities for the upcoming day. Each day the spacecraft would send back all of its data from the previous day—images, spectroscopic results, and vehicle telemetry. While the rovers slept through the Martian night, scientist would review and, in domain specific groups (such as "atmospheric" or "geology"), formulate what they would like to do during the following day. These groups came together to propose the next day's activities and negotiate for the limited resources within each sol. Next they would start to develop a plan which was turned into a sequence the spacecraft could understand; this plan was ultimately transmitted to each rover for execution the following day.

Each of these steps was supported with a collection of applications, including several core tools and a handful of scripts. The systems in place for the mission were some of the specific tools that had been reviewed and redesigned by the HCI group, offering a unique opportunity for the designers: the chance to provide day to day (and sometimes night to night) support for the set of applications whose design they had a hand in, directly in the context of use. Accepting this opportunity, one of the team members was staffed on the mission in the role of Tactical Application Planner Support.

To say that they learned more than they could have imagined about the domain, the users, and their goals would be an understatement. Working day to day with planners, scientists and mission managers provided a spectacularly rich set of data, all of which the designers are currently working to fold into the next generation of data browsing and tactical planning software for interplanetary robotic exploration. But more importantly, this level of integration built trust, established credibility, and fostered relationships that have proven invaluable in the ongoing efforts; designers developed close working relationships with the team tasked with developing the next generation of software tools, which made tight integration possible (and successful) during this current development effort. They also succeeded in conveying the value of applying iterative design processes to the mission managers, many of whom are critical stakeholders (and understandably protective gatekeepers for future user access) in upcoming missions. It's important to remember how critical it is to recognize opportunities like these as a medium in which to convey the value of iterative design, and to take advantage of them.

The rovers are still chugging along, with Spirit and Opportunity still conducting science 12 times longer than their expected lives! This extended mission is now providing a test-bed for the designers and developers to test concepts being implemented for the next generation tools mentioned earlier. Soon after the rovers entered their "extended missions" (the time after that initial 90 days), developers began to contemplate ways to improve the tools and development practices at the same time. The HCI Group, having established both credibility and professional relationships with the developers, became collaborators in this new effort almost from the outset.

Designers, particularly those working in complex technical domains, should likewise never underestimate the power of data in establishing credibility for your design decisions. The Ames HCI Group, having spent time supporting the teams developing the support software used to organize evidentiary data in the Columbia Accident investigation, became interested in the systems used to collect data generated during mission anomalies. Anomalies, in this sense, refer to anything, good or bad, occurring during a mission that is unexpected. In many cases, anomalies are the precursors for mishaps. By studying these events, systems could be designed to support their collection in a way that standardized procedures and expanded the searchable data agency wide.

Through the support of the center's Chief Engineer, the HCI Group gained significant access to observe anomaly data collection in a variety of settings, and mission phases. Significant time and resources were invested collecting data using Beyer and Holtzblatt's Contextual Inquiry methodology. At the conclusion of this inquiry, the resulting models, process analyses, and prototypes were presented to the Chief Engineer, and subsequently, to the missions who participated in the observations, and finally, funding managers at NASA Headquarters. The credibility this data lent to the design decisions based on it made a powerful case for the creation of such systems, and ultimately, led to a significant funding decision as Ames is now tasked with replacing the existing anomaly resolution infrastructure based at least in part on this work.

Prototyping

If you only have one card to play when trying to appeal to the sensibilities of engineers, scientists, or developers, your safest bet is clearly "data." While the styles of these different groups can be as varied as flakes of snow, their view of data is consistent: data drive so much of what these folks do from day to day that it provides at least a common starting point for your conversation. While they might not always concur with your data, at least it provides a common ground—a framework, and language, within which you can reach consensus.

At the same time, it's important to bring the right data to the party. Prototyping is commonly defined as either low or high fidelity—but this binary set of descriptors barely scratches the surface of the range of fidelity possibilities. In "Breaking the Fidelity Barrier" (McCurdy, Connors, Pyrzak, Kanefsky, and Vera, CHI 2006) the authors described five dimensions along which fidelity can vary, from low to high:

— Visual Fidelity
— Depth
— Breadth
— Interactivity
— Data Fidelity[21]

Prototypes can be high or low fidelity visually—hand drawn vs. pixel accurate renderings. The navigation can be high or low fidelity in terms of breadth or depth. They can also have high or low fidelity interactivity, and perhaps most importantly, high or low fidelity data, where high fidelity data might represent an actual data set and low fidelity data might be a few spoofed data elements—"lorem ipsum" rather than actual text, for example.

The advent of portable data formats such as XML has really opened the floodgates for high fidelity data models underlying otherwise low fidelity artifacts. Why might one go to the trouble to use a high fidelity data set? A good example to consider might be the Cable TV or PVR channel guide; it's all well and good for designers to propose flashy fully labeled lickable candy-tiles when considering the 10 shows the designer might include in their comps, but it's another thing to see that treatment in a display of 400 channels where many of the programming items might be only 30 minutes long and therefore too small to support a 50+ character label. In this example the context supplied by using the real data set might immediately illuminate the successes and "opportunities" within the design, and calls attention to the lack of scalability of the proposed design.

This demonstrates the variety of data you can collect by varying your prototypes along these five axes. A low visual fidelity prototype with high fidelity depth can help evaluators elicit user responses to an entire process through an artifact (such as a start to finish ATM transaction). Series of screens with high visual fidelity but low fidelity along the other dimensions are often used to gather reactions to the look and feel of a product. To gather data about users' ability to interact with the system, and the scalability of the data representations, it would be useful to select high fidelity along the interactivity and data fidelity dimensions when designing and assembling a mixed fidelity prototype.

Nothing will assuage a developer's fears that a designer has proposed a solution that isn't scalable or understandable faster than *data showing the scalability and effectiveness* of an interface demonstrated through user tests of an artifact based on real data.

The HCI Group at Ames took exactly this approach when designing the next generation of tools for Robotic Surface operations. Once the set of all current plans (both as planned and as executed) had been captured in XML, it took very little effort for one (talented) developer to create a range of prototypes demonstrating new visualizations and interactive methods that operated on the real MER data. Using this mixed fidelity prototype, the authors were able to conduct ongoing tests with actual users of the system without ever having to make excuses for using simulated data. Users also were able to focus on the interactions and the visualizations rather

21   McCurdy, Connors, Pyrzak, Kanefsky and Vera, CHI 2006

than irregularities in the data presented (since there were none), and they were looking at the same data they were using in their production systems in nearly real-time.

By carefully selecting these two dimensions to focus on in our mixed fidelity prototype, our team was able to gather detailed data on a timed task—something that would be impossible without the high fidelity data and interactions. This sort of data, presented in the context of development triage, makes particularly compelling arguments (especially if the audience has a healthy skepticism with respect to design processes).

What have we learned?

The industry has changed quite a bit in the last 8 years. Interaction Design, and the design disciplines in general, have enjoyed quite a surge in acceptance and popularity—call it our own "iPod Halo effect." The success of well-designed products from OXO, Apple, Volkswagen, Target, and others has opened the eyes of engineers and accountants in a variety of industries. However, like any relatively new discipline that finds itself in demand, we must take care to integrate ourselves into existing organizations and processes—swim with the tide (or in some cases, the riptide) rather than against it. There is little likelihood of this integration if we cannot foster trust while instigating and sustaining interdisciplinary communication.

There's perhaps a cautionary tale for design practitioners to consider: recall the introduction of Information Technology into the corporate infrastructure in the late 50s and early 60s. In those days computers were mysterious props from the set of science fiction movies, accompanied by somewhat vague promises of increased efficiency and worker productivity.

They were installed into special semi-hermetic, starkly lit white rooms behind glass windows, and serviced by white-robed acolytes. Eventually many organizations' IT departments became focused more on their own growth and self-perpetuation rather than whatever the broader goals of their companies. The result is still felt—IT departments frequently at odds with business managers, and endless deployments of newer and larger internal projects—many of which are consistently ranked by their own users as failures.

How can we as design practitioners avoid a similar fate? By fostering trust with external teams, stakeholders, and users, using any and all means at our disposal. Of course it's not always possible to find yourself staffed on the teams you are building tools for, but there are almost always opportunities for contextual observation, and we've found users relish the opportunity to have a voice in the design process.

Another approach designers can adopt is supporting design decisions, where possible, with data. It is important that design decisions be set in an empirical context rather than at the "whim of that designer person."

Finally, despite having worked in a range of development environments, the one thing that consistently works well is the close integration of design resources within development teams. This includes having designers participate in bug/feature priority setting, and having design issues assigned to them as "bugs" or feature requests within the broader development tracking mechanism. By becoming part of this broader engineering team, the interPersonal relationships—and trust—are forged and solidified.

By consistently articulating and applying a design process, generating and maintaining credibility, and judiciously using prototypes of varying and often mixed fidelity to convey design intent, designers have more opportunities than ever to bring design practice into organizations—organizations that are newly receptive to design application, and are eagerly anticipating the results.

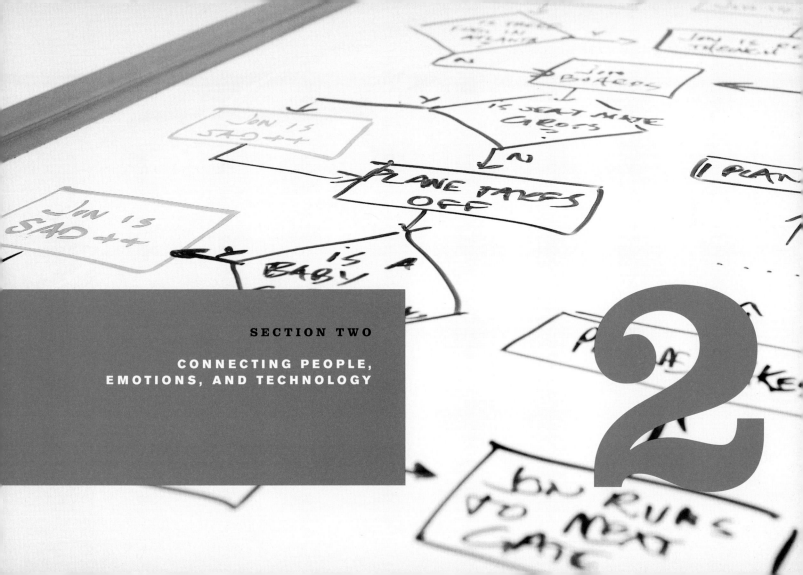

SECTION TWO

CONNECTING PEOPLE,
EMOTIONS, AND TECHNOLOGY

2

The dialogue of Interaction Design exists between a person and a product, system, or service. This dialogue is both physical and emotional in nature, and is manifested in form, function, and technology. While Interaction Designers frequently work on projects related to computing, the field in and of itself has nothing inherently to do with computers. Instead, the field is best thought of in terms of a methodology, and the major contribution an Interaction Designer can provide in a business setting is a strong process that connects people, technology, and the emotional qualities of sensory data (generally pertaining to aesthetics). One can consider the results of this process as the *design of human behavior*. The methodology is usually characterized by several distinct phases. For example, an Interaction Design project may begin with understanding, move to a phase of generative synthesis, progress through creation and testing, and end with implementation or "execution."

Usable, useful, and desirable

Many practitioners engaged in human-centered design activities have adopted the platitude that designed products should be "usable, useful, and desirable". Liz Sanders, former Vice President at Fitch Richardson-Smith, coined this phrase in an effort to illustrate the necessity of converging perspectives in research.[22] The three terms are closely linked, but each implies a quite separate facet of design. While many reference these three traits as goals of design activities, it is rare to find a product that fulfills two of the three characteristics; a product that touches all three is a rare gem of design.

Usable implies a strong and close connection between the functionality of the product and the abilities of the end user. People—or "users," in a more clinical sense—have limits that impede their ability to perform. These limits include memory, perception, and cognition. Many are innate, and rarely do users consider the boundaries (or existence) of these limitations. Nor should they—most people are busy enough without having to consider how many units may be currently stored in short-term memory or how bright a stimulus is shining. Usable implies that users can understand the purpose of a product, can form strong understandings of how the product will work for them, and can deduce how to go about manipulating the product in order to achieve a goal. Very often, usability is tied to learnability: How quickly can one understand a novel system? Additionally, usability is frequently judged according to metrics such as "number of errors" or "time on task." This is statistically relevant data when considering a system as technology, but clearly does little to address or track the more emotional issues of happiness or joy.

Useful generally refers to the match between a system's functionality and the goals the user has in mind. Goals can be thought of as end results that someone may wish to accomplish. Products provide utility only when they allow the user to successfully meet the requirements he has (implicitly or explicitly) defined. For example, a user may wish to write a letter to all of the friends he has not communicated with in "a long time." An email system may or may not provide an easy way to accomplish this goal. If the system behaves in a usable fashion, but simply does not allow

---

22   The phrase "usable, useful, and desirable" was first presented in a Design Management Institute article authored by Liz Sanders. The article was entitled "Converging Perspectives: Product Development Research for the 1990s", in Vol 3, No 4, Fall, 1992.

this user to achieve this task, it has not proven to be useful. Computers are bad at dealing with human utterances like "a long time," yet humans achieve a great deal of usefulness out of these ill-formed phrases. Usefulness is often considered after the fact, as marketing attempts to persuade us that we require more utility in our lives. Advertising pitches features of a product, and packaging of consumer electronics frequently alludes to the *number* of features. While the naïve may be persuaded by a large number of functions presented by a product, some quickly learn that all of the functionality in the world is useless if the *useful* functions aren't present.

Desirability is the fleeting idea associated with emotions—that a product may successfully fill an emotional, or subjective (and often superficial) niche within an audience. Physical product designers—or Industrial Designers—have long understood the importance of creating objects of beauty and desire. Consider the extra amount of money someone may pay for a Jaguar or a BMW. While the engine is probably superior to that of a Honda of a Ford, most users will rarely venture under the hood to find out. Instead, the aesthetic—or sensory experience—of the vehicle appeals to users on a level that is innate, passionate, and frequently illogical.

This section describes the three facets of Interaction Design, and the Interaction Design process. It begins with a discussion of the procedural focus of Interaction Design as it pertains to designing what people want and need. The role of intuition is examined as compared to the necessity for ethnographic user research. This is followed by an investigation into the role aesthetics plays in the development of Interaction Design solutions, specifically with regard to brand and identity. Finally, the role technology plays in the development of Interaction Design solutions is examined, with attention placed on the relatively new subfield of Information Architecture as applied to the design of technology-driven products.

3

CHAPTER THREE: A PROCESS FOR THINKING ABOUT PEOPLE

define	discover	synthesize	construct	refine	reflect
• team building • technical assessment • hypothesize	• contexts • benchmarking • user needs	• process maps • opportunity map • frameworks • personas • scenarios	• features and functions • behavior • design language • interactions and flow models • collaborative design	• evaluation • scoping • interaction • specification	• post mortem • opportunity map • benchmarking • market acceptance

Research knowledge production by phase

• prototypical user
  model
• prototypical user
  needs
• client's needs
	• user mental models
	• user process models
	• user's relation to context
	• summary of current
	  products meeting
	  needs (lite review)
		• relationships needs
		  of users, client, and
		  context
		• identify gaps
		  (opportunities for new
		  product or service)
			• examples of process and flow models that users
			  will and will not accept
			• insights into high level guidelines for interaction
			• evaluation of widget performance and its
			  relationship to software reuse
			• improved interaction flow models
				• opportunites for
				  improving design process
				• acceptance of design in
				  the market place
				• new assessment of gaps
				  (opportunities for new
				  products and services)

Zimmerman, Evenson, Forlizzi
Design Process

Interaction Design is a creative process focused on people. A number of well-known designers and academics have examined the commonalities across design processes as applied by various consultancies, and have unrolled a distinct set of patterns that illustrate the movement of a design from conception through creation. These patterns explain the discrete steps that are taken when developing a cohesive Interaction Design solution. It is important to emphasize, however, that these steps are rarely delineated as carefully as they are described below. Instead, the designer works in a certain haze or fog—both lost within the trees but always aware, on some unconscious level, of the forest.

The process of design

John Zimmerman, Shelley Evenson, and Jodi Forlizzi, of the School of Design at Carnegie Mellon University, have presented a formal framework for discovering and extracting knowledge during the design process.[23] This framework includes six core components, each building upon the previous

23   Zimmerman, J., Forlizzi, J., and Evenson, S. "Taxonomy for Extracting Design Knowledge from Research Conducted During Design Cases." Originally published in Futureground 04 (Conference of the Design Research Society) Proceedings, Melbourne, Australia, November 2004, available as CD-rom.

and each requiring a unique set of skills and tools. These components are named Define, Discover, Synthesize, Construct, Refine, and Reflect, and are discussed below.[24]

Defining the design problem or opportunity

Definition occurs in an effort to understand the problem space. Frequently, designers will receive a design brief that includes vocabulary or references to particular work already conducted. For example, a designer may be explicitly given the task of redesigning the interface of a printer, in order to make it easier to use or to take into account new functionality that has been developed. At this phase in the process, the designer's role is one of skeptical visionary—he is able to "feel" the outcome of the project, yet is often unsure of what exactly needs to be done at all. To objectify this feeling, the designer may explicitly list questions relating to the task: Does the interface need to be redesigned? Is the new functionality useful? Who are the stakeholders in the project? The designer attempts to understand wants and needs, and to balance political requirements with implied end user demands and business goals. The process of human-centered design relies heavily on modeling target users in an effort to create a prototypical audience for design. A model is a representation of a real thing, and a

model of a user is a representation of a real person. A basic form of model that has been embraced by Interaction Designers and is created in the initial stages of a project is the Persona.

Author and designer Alan Cooper has defined Personas as the hypothetical individuals that take on the characteristics of real users. To create a Persona, one may simply "develop a precise description of our user and what he wishes to accomplish."[25] This Persona seems to come to life during the development stages of a project, and gives all of the members of a design team a common goal to focus on: pleasing a demanding, albeit fake, individual. A Persona usually takes the form of several paragraphs of text, followed by images that illustrate lifestyle choices, brands, and other physical embodiments of values. This stereotyping is at once highly specific yet subtly generic. It attempts to capture individual nuances and peculiarities, yet blend these nuances into a single individual.

Creating a Persona that is believable is difficult. Charming this Persona into life is even harder. It is easy to inadvertently produce a shallow, superficial representation of a group of people, and this representation only serves to reinforce existing—and often inaccurate—stereotypes. But if one is able to create a good Persona, a description that is backed by actual research and that celebrates the unique qualities of the target audience, the value of the Persona as a method becomes dramatically clear. The Persona begins to become an active member of the design team, and questions can be answered not by asking "what would the user want" or "what does marketing require," but instead, "What does Jill (our

---

24 Zimmerman, John, Forlizzi, Jodi, and Evenson, Shelley. "Taxonomy for Extracting Design Knowledge from Research Conducted During Design Cases." Originally published in Futureground 2004 (Conference of the Design Research Society) Proceedings, Melbourne, Australia, November 2004. It is interesting to note the commonalities of word choice in defining design process. The six components described by the CMU researchers are highly similar in nature to IDEO's four-step process (Observation, Brainstorming, Prototyping, Implementation), Design Edge's three-step process (Define, Discover, Develop), or Smart Design's three steps (Conceive, Create, Complete). This may indicate the propensity for designers to try to define what they do—which implies that what it is they do is, actually, quite messy and difficult to define at all.

25 Cooper, Alan. *The Inmates Are Running the Asylum: Why High Tech Products Drive Us Crazy and How to Restore the Sanity*. Sams, 1999. p123.

Persona) truly need?" If an engineer begins to ask these questions, he has, essentially, embraced the notion of designing for humanity rather than for technology.

It is important that the details of a Persona extend outside of the given "problem statement." That is, when researching printers, a designer doesn't simply analyze Jill's printer. Instead, it becomes important to focus on and begin to understand other facets of Jill: her car, her food preferences, and the types of shows she watches on television. In fact, by modeling everything about Jill *except* her printer, the design team begins to paint a vivid picture of brand, style, and behavior which can be synthesized during interpretation.

It is also critical to remember that the Persona cannot be established on a whim. As the Persona creates an archetypical understanding of the target audience, all efforts should be made to ensure that it is backed by reality. Traditional user-research can, and should, inform the creation of the Persona.

One of the simplest yet most powerful tools available to Interaction Designers is the written word. Language affords a host of capabilities, including the act of persuasion and rich description. When used to organize information, the written word can be used to create narratives of use that explain the proper and expected use of a system. A good Persona is rich with detail and is thus predictable, in the same way that one can predict the actions of a friend or loved one. While these predictions may not be right all of the time, it is possible to anticipate with some degree of accuracy what an individual will do in a given situation. The accuracy improves over time—a long-term relationship provides intimate insight into how people approach problems or situations. The same is true for Personas. By

Persona: **Jill Farington**, 27 years old. An earth-friendly poet.

Jill is a twenty-seven year old baker at a local bakery in Portland, Oregon. She claims to be a vegetarian, but will often try the salmon at dinner. She likes to bake as it makes her feel productive; she gains a sense of control over the kitchen, and the outcome of her actions is fairly obvious and tangible. She spends a bit of time on the internet searching for new vegan-friendly baking techniques, and although she doesn't like using her cell phone, she carries it with her everywhere to make sure she can get in touch with her friends and family. She always remembers to turn it off before Yoga class.

Jill uses an old digital camera to take photographs of her baked goods. The camera takes lousy pictures, and Jill is starting to look for a newer model. She doesn't have any interest in technology or in the features and functions presented to her on the various boxes, but she cares a lot about the way her bread is visually captured. She also needs a really simple way to catalog her images on her computer, as she takes pictures of her creations daily.

Barefoot Yoga Co.   Tazo Tea   Chuck Taylors

Timbuk2 Designs   Patagonia   Trek Bicycles

American Apparel   Sierra Trading Post   Burt's Bees

Five Wishes

"I wish I understood how to open my own bakery; I've played with the numbers, but I just can't figure out how to make it profitable."

"I wish there was a camera that wasn't made in Chinese sweatshops; I don't feel comfortable supporting that kind of work."

"I'm sick of hearing about technology and how much I need it. I need less technology in my life, not more."

"I wish big companies would start making things for me; I feel like most of the things I buy are for other people, and I'm not supposed to like them."

"I wish I had more time in my day for relaxing."

Decision Making and Values

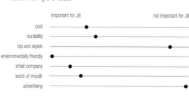

An example of a Persona

"living" with these Personas, the designer can begin to predict what these hypothetical people will do in novel situations. These predictions can be used prior to a system ever existing, and can be used to create visionary and compelling rationales for new ideas. They can also be used to assist in understanding and revising existing systems, and to structure scenarios of use that articulate goals, tasks, and actions.

Engineers have formalized these scenarios and often refer to them as "Use Cases," in an effort to relate these written descriptions to "Test Cases" (systematic bug testing to ensure a piece of code is operating correctly). A modeling language (UML) has emerged to help visualize these Use Cases in a diagrammatic format. Yet the formality of these methods is a peculiarity that is useful but not necessary. A written scenario can also be thought of as a narrative essay, as it provides narration through a particular situation. It is, however, most usefully thought of as a story of the above Persona using a product to achieve a goal. This presupposes that the product exists (it usually doesn't) and implies that the design team understands a great deal about what the Persona will want to do.

The use of scenario-based product development has several core benefits. Narrative allows designers to contemplate the more human side of their creations—rather than focusing on technology, narrative shifts the emphasis to one of creative learning, problem solving, or attaining a goal. As behavior exists in the fourth dimension, these scenarios become

sketches of time. Industrial Designers and Graphic Designers can quickly explain the value of visual sketching in their design process: Sketching is a problem-solving tool, used not simply to visualize ideas but to actually discover and generate a large number of solutions to a problem.

In the same way, the act of building a scenario is useful as a *generative tool for discovering new ideas*. The scenario, quite simply, becomes the Interaction Designer's napkin sketch. In the same way that a drawing has specific attributes that contribute to its success (perspective, line weight, tone, content), a scenario too has several critical components that aid in comprehension.

First, a scenario needs to include a product and a person. In the early stages of Interaction Design development, the product may not actually exist yet. The scenario development is also a form of product development. The product may be thought of as an ambiguous shape or a piece of information space; it need not be concrete.

Next, a compelling story is created that includes precise detail, sensory awareness, and vivid descriptors. Precision implies an exacting, accurate, and well-defined point of view. When combined with detail, the audience receives a comprehensive and thorough verbal discussion. Sensory awareness adds issues of sight, sound, and touch; paints an image of a smell; and may include (in rare cases) issues of taste. Vivid descriptors create colorful and dramatic emotional responses. The elements present in a story include a plot, characters, a setting, a climax, and an ending. These are also the major elements in a movie or in a television show, and create the general formulaic essence of storytelling. Finally, the guiding principles of a compelling story include a point of view and the overarching goal of the story.

Explaining to your boss that you are going to require several weeks to write stories is a hard sell. Interaction Designers have developed various formalities associated with scenario writing in order to emphasize the business-relevance of their creations. These may include matrices with formal variables described (including Actors, Goals, Tasks, Benefits, and Supporting Functions), or more formal step-by-step breakdowns of tasks into task flow charts. The essence of these creations is, however, the same: to humanize a situation and illustrate a cohesive vision of product use over time.

Discovering hidden wants, needs, and desires

After the definition phase, designers attempt to gather data relating to the given problem. The next step in the design process, Discovery, is often lacking in many corporations and consultancies due to tight budgets and poor understanding of the value presented by this phase. Discovery in-volves understanding wants and needs, and accumulating artifacts related to the defined opportunity. Traditional approaches to design emphasize aesthetic qualities related to craft, beauty, and form. The solution to a problem of design is judged based on emotional value, and the judgment—or critique—is often grounded in the field of fine art. Interaction Design, however, shifts the focus from the visual to the human. A design solution is judged based on the relevance to the individual who ultimately must use the creation. Central to understanding this principle is embracing a very simple idea, but an idea that dramatically refocuses the locus of attention during the act of creation. This idea is that The User Is Not Like Me.[26]

When embraced by designers, this core philosophy implies that consumers are unique, and that all members of the product development team hold a bias in the form of an expert blind spot. The more one knows about a topic, the more one forgets what it is like *not to know*. Expertise makes it nearly impossible to remember what it is like to be a novice.

To illustrate this point, consider an example. You are the designer working on a kiosk for a bus station. The kiosk will replace the need for constant assistance from on-staff personnel (thus saving a fair amount of money), and will allow riders to purchase tickets even during the "off hours." Your work has been extensive, and in the process of development, you have become an expert on busses, kiosks, and interfaces relating to these walk-up-and-use systems. In the end, you feel you have designed a

---

26 I credit Professor Bonnie John of Carnegie Mellon University as developing this subtle mantra. While others have certainly realized that they are designing for someone unlike them, Professor John engrained this phrase in the heads of students in the Human Computer Interaction Institute, creating several generations of designers and engineers who truly believe in user-centered design.

pretty great kiosk. It has a lot of features, and even allows the tracking of a complicated route with multiple destinations and layovers in various cities. The kiosk comes to fruition, and slowly finds a home in various southern cities.

Now consider Dana Jones, a single mother of two who has just been displaced by a large hurricane that hit the southern United States. Before the hurricane, Dana worked at a small hotel. She was in charge of the general office management, and was responsible for nearly all of the accounting and bill paying. Dana didn't go to college. She taught herself the relevant software programs, and while she doesn't understand all of the laws and regulations she needs to follow, she prides herself on making very few mistakes. She has no extended family. She managed, quite successfully, to locate a beautiful and affordable historic house for her two children, but it has been destroyed in the storm. She has no renter's insurance, and was living month to month prior to the disaster. Dana's credit cards are overextended and were destroyed in the hurricane, as was nearly everything else she owns. She doesn't know where she is going to take the kids. She's been told, however, that she needs to evacuate the city immediately, and the bus is the only affordable and immediate way out.

When Dana uses your interactive kiosk, what state of mind will she have? Will she be happy and easy going? Does she hope that the kiosk will be riddled with features, and that she will be able to map her route in a visual manner—zooming in on various landmarks along the way, and saving her route to a personal account?

The User Is Not Like Me. In Dana's particular situation, she is about as unlike you as you may ever wish. Are you responsible for the interaction Dana has, in her unlikely and unpredictable situation? In order to understand that The User Is Not Like Me, Interaction Designers practice a form of user research that draws heavily on the fields of Anthropology and the social sciences, yet encourages and emphasizes the richness of the individual over the demographic style of quantitative research commonly utilized by marketers.

Ethnography can be considered a qualitative description of the human social condition, based on fieldwork and observation. This human condition implies that social phenomenon occur within a culture, and exist when there is interaction between individuals. Anthropologist Bronislaw Malinowski is generally considered to be the first to embrace the notion of actually observing, in person, the interaction between individuals. During World War I, Malinowski observed the native culture of Papua by immersing himself in this island culture and documenting the results in the text *Argonauts of the Western Pacific*. Malinowski's methodology was unique in that he used firsthand observation to document and analyze daily occurrences—Malinowski can be thought of as the first to utilize participant observation as an anthropological technique.[27]

Participant observation is an important aspect of Interaction Design, as it formally acknowledges that a product does not exist in a rational and substantial way until it is considered by society. Simply producing a beautiful, useful, or cost-effective item does not guarantee success. The product needs to fit appropriately into the culture in which it is to be used and sold. This is a core distinction between design and fine art. While fine art may be appreciated in the eye of the beholder, the artwork can be considered successful *upon creation* (or when the *artist* deems it finished). The piece

27 Malinowski, Bronislaw. *Argonauts of the Western Pacific.* Waveland Press, Reprint Edition, 1984.

of artwork—and the artist—still creates a sense of dialogue with the user, but the dialogue is completely unconstrained. Conversely, design cannot truly be considered successful until the *user* considers it finished—*on consumption*. The dialogue has a much deeper set of constraints placed upon it, and good design will help the user engage in that conversation fluidly.

Ethnographic tools used by Interaction Designers attempt to understand what people do and why they do it. The first is easy to determine; the latter is tremendously difficult to discern. People have a very hard time explaining why they do the things they do, and human behavior often seems illogical when considered by an impartial observer. Therefore, interpretation—making meaning of gathered data—plays a critical role in translating research into valuable design criteria. This act of interpretation is one of the primary differences in skill between a designer and a marketer. Interpretation often requires a leap of faith (or an intuitive jump from one point to another), and while the designer (as artist) learns to trust this intuition, the marketer (as businessman) is frequently taught to doubt or ignore it. While the latter may end up with a more sound argument, the former may be in a better place to truly empathize with the target audience.

Most ethnographic tools are generally poor methods of determining if someone would buy a certain product, identifying how much someone would pay for a certain product, and understanding what color, texture, material, size, or shape to make a certain product. While tools like surveys or interviews can certainly ask questions relating to these details, people have a difficult time in estimating or remembering details related to this type of preference. Instead, ethnography helps designers identify problems with existing designs (understanding the nuances of product usage); understand how people work, play, and live; and identify *why* people do the things they do with a product, service, or system. A basic premise of anthropology is that context shapes a great deal of factors in society, and the same holds true when considering the "society" of the workplace or the home. One form of ethnography that emphasizes the importance of understanding work in its natural environment is called Contextual Inquiry.

A Contextual Inquiry is similar to an interview, but recognizes how heavily an awareness of the workplace conditions will affect and inform action. Ethnographers Hugh Beyer and Karen Holtzblatt have identified four key principles of Contextual Inquiry. [28] These principles help emphasize that the User Is Not Like Me. The principles of focus, context, partnership, and interpretation allow the Interaction Designer to truly understand the hidden work structures—and hidden needs and desires—in a target audience.

Everyone has a point of view. The problem with a point of view is that it both reveals and conceals. When one approaches a problem with a particular direction already established, it is difficult to have an "open mind" to changes that may take place. However, the opposite is equally as difficult: Approaching a problem with a truly clean slate is nearly impossible. Focus is the acknowledged pre-set view of what is going to be addressed through the ethnographic inquiry. It gives the designers a central topic to attend to and a statement to rally around. This statement can be thought

28   Holtzblatt, Karen, and Hugh Beyer. *Contextual Design : A Customer-Centered Approach to Systems Designs.* Morgan Kaufmann, 1997.

of as the focus statement, and is particularly relevant when trying to articulate the reason behind the research. A focus statement takes the conceptual approach of framing the inquiry.

For example, when conducting research intended to investigate and understand the various tools used in a print shop, any of the following foci may apply:

1. "The focus of our research is to understand the process of creating a printed document"
2. "The focus of our research is to understand the complexity of the tools used in creating a printed document in order to simplify the process for the designer"
3. "The focus of our research is to examine the individual printing and binding tools used by the designer in the creation of a printed document, with a particular emphasis on ink, consumables, and maintenance."

The statements become increasingly more specific, and this specificity will provide the design team with much more detailed information. However, this detail is at the expense of the larger, system wide view. Generating a focus statement, then, must be tied to a higher goal or a set of strategic project statements. These statements, often mandated by a client or an executive, can assist in the directional goals of research in context.

Context implies the interrelated conditions in which work occurs. This principle is the easiest to embrace on a theoretical level, but hardest to implement on a pragmatic level. To understand context, go to the place where work occurs: Go to the users, rather than bringing the users to you, and watch what they do as they conduct *real work*. So simple, yet so evasive!

Consider again the previous example: You are an Interaction Designer working on the development of a printer interface. You want to view context, in order to truly understand how people go about printing with their existing tools. This knowledge will give you good ideas of how people print, and also will provide insight into problems that exist with existing printers. Can you creep into a print shop and watch a designer go about her day? How can you be sure that she will be using the printer during the time you spend at the office—what if she chooses to sketch things by hand instead? And consider the amount of preparation required to get into that office for the one or two minutes of printing. Is it worth your time to travel all the way to the office, get your recording equipment set up, and wait for printing to occur—just to watch someone press a few buttons?

The answer is emphatically *yes*. It is worth your time, and it is tremendously difficult to rationalize *why* it is worth your time—especially to a skeptical manager who demands that you remain billable, and to a client who is, ultimately, billed. Context offers fodder for innovation. Hidden in the physical work space, in the users' words, and in the tools they use are the beautiful gems of knowledge that can create revolutionary, breakthrough products or simply fix existing, broken products. People do strange things—unexpected things—and being there to witness and record these minute and quick moments of humanity is simply invaluable to the product development process. These details trigger design insights, and the equally important rationale to back up design decisions to other members of the design team.

Once you have arrived in the physical context, or the environment where work is done, it may seem logical to remain quiet and observe the work as it occurs. Most people assume that they will disrupt the "natural" flow of work and wish to remain as unobtrusive as possible. As the goal of a Contextual Inquiry is to gather as much rich data as possible, it is important to reject this logic and become an active participant in the inquiry. This participation takes the form of partnership, and is likened to that of a master and apprentice in the days of guilds. An apprentice did not sit quietly and observe. He became engaged, and tried things, and questioned things, and assisted in the process. When observing people printing in a print shop, it is imperative to ask questions. "Why are you doing that? Is that what you expect to happen? What are you doing now? Can I try it?" Experience is a guide to better understand when to ask questions and when to remain quiet, but a master and apprentice relationship will allow an investigator to best understand the nuances of work and truly gain the confidence of the participant being observed.

Interpretation, or the assignment of meaning to fact, is a subjective form of synthesis. It is also the most critical part of the Contextual Inquiry process, and the portion of the process that is ignored with the most frequency. The probable reason this principle is tossed aside? Put bluntly, interpretation is difficult. To interpret data is to ask question after question, making assumption upon assumption, always getting towards the heart of the largest question of all: *Why do people do the things they do?* Interpretation occurs in context, but the critical interpretation often occurs back in the "lab"—in the design studio, while the designer is sketching or the engineer is building, or in a meeting where data is passed around in nicely printed binders. Interpretation is qualitative, and can be wrong. This makes

for a difficult combination when trying to justify design decisions. However, interpretation is a creative form of synthesis, and provides a smooth and elegant transition between Discovery and the actual generative form of design. A strong interpretation session combining various techniques of data aggregation can yield tremendous results.

Frequently, interpretation occurs in the head of the designer. This "moment of epiphany" may be thought of in the shower or scrawled on the back of a napkin. The Interaction Designer understands the importance of structuring this interpretation into a repeatable and formal process, and a *good* Interaction Designer is able to communicate not only the pragmatic interpretation but also the necessity of interpretation.

Marketing frequently participates in the Discovery phase of a project. In many companies, Marketing will actually *conduct* the entire Discovery phase of a project before ever asking for assistance from Design. Thus, on the surface, Interaction Design and Marketing seem to have a great deal in common. Both fields are interested in human behavior. Both fields care about brand, and presentation, and understanding the value in human experience with products. The interpretation of gathered data, however, is dramatically different across disciplines. Marketing relies heavily on gathered opinions and generalizations that can be made across a demographic, while Interaction Design cares primarily about actual behavior (often of the few rather than the many).

A common data-gathering technique used by marketing firms has been the focus group. This method, combined with questionnaires and competitive analysis, creates the core set of tools used to gather opinions, wants, and needs from end users. A typical marketing firm may poll an Internet message board, a group of volunteers, or shoppers at the mall to find out their feelings about existing and novel products. This appears, on the surface, to be strongly user centered and to be a useful way of understanding purchasing trends. While the method can certainly be applied properly, it is also quite easy to misuse or misinterpret the results of a focus group.

A successful focus group depends on a successful moderator. This requires an individual who is unbiased, creative, has the capacity for empathy and can understand and gauge the direction and flow of conversation quickly—and adapt to unforeseen circumstances. This is a rare individual, and while many who hold an MBA may have several of these skills, few can claim the entire host of abilities. A focus group depends on a compelling and continual discussion among six to eight people—people who may share similar traits, but usually have never met each other before. In a group of this size, there will most likely be personality differences—some differences of the magnitude that can absolutely destroy the "value" of the entire experience. These differences may include vocal distinctions (someone may simply be louder than the rest) or morale oppositions (people may get into conflict over root issues of ethics and proper behavior). Worst of all, however, is the apathetic focus group—the members whom are willing to be persuaded, pulled, and shaped by the rest of the group. In a situation like this, gathered data will not only be poor, it will frequently reflect the opposite of the truth, and it will most likely be thrown out during analysis.

Most important, poorly run focus groups will highlight hypothetical behavior. A naïve facilitator may ask questions pertaining to opinions, and encourage people to consider what they *would* do or *would* buy. In a hypothetical situation with fake money, people may be more willing to "purchase" anything—and would most likely pay a lot more in false currency than they would when their wallet is open. These hypothetical opinions rarely translate directly into behavior.[29] Thus, the value of the data gathered from a focus group is entirely dependent on the ability of the moderator; perhaps those engaged in design activities are more capable of engaging users in this type of study than are marketers.

Ethnography performed during the Discovery phase of the design process should be user focused rather than competitively driven. A competitive analysis, or competitive product benchmarking, is a method used to understand the similarities and differences between products that have already been released. The outcome of this technique traditionally includes the creation of a competitive matrix of products, highlighting trends related to features and functions.

While this is a valuable tool for understanding strategic marketplace positioning, it is frequently performed *instead* of ethnography, user testing, needs analysis, or a more formal product evaluation. This is problematic for a number of reasons. First, the emphasis of the competitive analysis is placed on features, rather than goals. By collecting and analyzing similarities in feature sets, the design team has implicitly embraced extra functionality as a goal for design. The quantity and scope of features, however, are nearly irrelevant to the user, who cares about more conceptual issues such as goals, tasks, and activities.

29 The late Jay Doblin, the founder of Doblin Inc. in Chicago, recalled an anecdote of just such a phenomenon: participants were asked to talk about and discuss a set of pens. Some of the pens were blue, and some were black, and the members of the focus group discussed at length why the black pen was simply superior in every way to the blue pen. After the discussion had ended, the participants were rewarded for their time by being allowed to take a pen for themselves as a "thank you" present. Sure enough—all of the participants selected the blue pens, leaving the "preferred" black ones behind.

An additional and larger implicit problem with relying solely on competitive product analysis, however, is the assumption that the features the competition has selected to include are the *right* features. The communication of product features and value throughout the production chain is so skewed *within* a company that comparing this value set *across* companies is a nearly useless exercise.

Consider the following anecdote as relayed to the author by a car dealer in Austin, Texas. A customer enters the dealership intent on purchasing a beige Ford Explorer. Ford has just sent the dealer a surplus of white Windstar minivans, and the dealer wants to move the inventory as quickly as possible, so the hard sell is on: "Wouldn't you prefer a nice white minivan instead?"

The customer reacts predictably: "Uhm, no, didn't you hear me? I want a Beige Explorer."

The dealer offers the minivan again, but this time at a significant discount. After all, he knows he can still make a profit even when he drops below MSRP, and he needs to get those Windstars off the lot. The discount is so deep, in fact, that the customer begins to change his mind. If the salesman is good enough, that customer may actually leave with a brand new white Windstar.

Now consider what happens at the end of the month, when the dealer reports his numbers to Ford Motor Company. White minivans are selling really, really well. The conclusion that is drawn by Ford, proper? Build more white minivans!

The internal channel communication of distribution and sales is murky and convoluted within a particular company. If the design team simply looks at the competition's features with the intention of copying them, the entire product segment begins to include that irrationally specified feature. And, sure enough, soon after the anecdote above was relayed, out came more white minivans from all of the other major vehicle manufacturers. The car industry is rich with examples like this. Consider how quickly the trend towards enormous SUVs blanketed the market, or how the need to brand an engine ("hemi") found its way through various companies. Thus, Discovery should be focused on understanding goals and tasks, rather than on features or functionality. Competitive analysis can be incredibly useful in understanding how competitors solved problems relating to user goals, and should be used in tandem with other techniques to emphasize these elements of design. The articulation of specific features will come later, and will be driven by user need rather than by the competitive offerings of other companies.

A cyclical process of synthesis, creation, and refinement

After Definition and Discovery, a designer begins an iterative cycle of Synthesis, Construction, and Refinement. These phases represent the most elusive and perhaps time-consuming aspects of the design process because they are the most dependent on experience, proliferation, and "talent." These phases, while highly intellectual, also require the "designer's intuition" and frequently rely on rapid ideation sketching, additional narrative development, and mind mapping as a generative method of problem solving and concept development. The designer creates a mass of ideas, testing them and gathering feedback, all the while honing in on a particular solution. The notion that a design occurs over time begins to illustrate one of the key distinctions between art and design. While an artist may enjoy sudden bursts of inspiration, a designer works through both a convergent and a divergent thought process of ideation. [30]

Convergent thinking attempts to locate the best answer—the optimum solution to a given problem. Engineers frequently practice a convergent set of thinking that focuses heavily on the need for a fast solution, a correct solution, and a logical solution. Designers too use this method of thought to hone in on a solution that can easily be presented to other stakeholders involved in the product development cycle. A solution occurring from a convergent thought process implicitly has some sort of "evidence" that makes it appear to be a proper route to follow, and it is familiar or safe in its "correctness." A good designer, however, balances convergent thinking with a healthy level of divergent thinking.

Divergent thought implies a great deal of risk. One must shift perspectives away from the safety of familiarity in order to explore what "could be." Author Richard Buchanan discusses the importance of shifting "placements" in order to encourage and assist in the development of innovation in design. Buchanan explains that "innovation comes when the initial selection is repositioned at another point in the framework, raising new questions and ideas." [31] He describes how signs, things, actions, and thoughts can be considered in light of one another in an effort to build new and creative ideas. Consider designing a new *thing*, such as a chair. Now shift the placement to imagine that chair as an *action*, or a *sign*, or a *thought*. This divergence away from the norm—a chair as an object—makes for wildly creative ideas of a chair as a service, or sitting as a philosophy; the notion of these placements, and their ability to be shifted, is what Buchanan refers to as the "quasi-subject matter of design thinking, from which the designer fashions a working hypothesis suited to special circumstances."

Divergent and Convergent thinking requires a mixture of analytical skills (logic, engineering, and the development of "appropriate solutions") and creative skills (drawing, mapping, "blue sky thinking"). This mixture is a rare but required duality that must exist in a successful designer. A designer will sketch, and think, and diagram, and write—and do these things over and over, each time refining and pruning away the "wrong" ideas in order to find the "right" one (convergent thinking in action). But wrong and right as applied to design are impossibly finite and are obviously the incorrect words. A designer may reject an idea as being "less good," as it does not fit well within the constrained design space, and may temporarily embrace a ridiculous idea that still fulfills the stated constraints or guidelines from the client. The constraints placed on the design are a mix of human, technical, and aesthetic boundaries. The difficulty lies in

---

30 Images of Jackson Pollack may come to mind. The late Pollack is one artist who has, through the production of difficult to understand paintings and several well-funded documentary films, come into the rather difficult role of attempting to explain painting to the masses. Many people claim not to understand art because they don't understand the literal fits of energy that went into the creation of Pollack's work. As design is frequently grouped with art, the repercussions of Pollack—and other expressionist and highly emotionally charged artists—may have had negative ripples throughout both product and Interaction Design.

31 Buchanan, Richard. "Wicked Problems in Design Thinking." *The Idea of Design.* Ed Victor Margolin and Richard Buchanan. MIT Press, 1996. p9.

discerning the hidden constraints, which the process itself helps uncover, and balancing these with the more explicit constraints, often defined by a client or a business executive.

In order to understand if the various creations have succeeded, it is important to test them with real people—people who represent the target audience—and to test not only their appeal but also their comprehensibility. Think Aloud Protocol (also referred to as Talking Aloud or simply User Testing) is an evaluation technique commonly used to understand problems people have with software interfaces. It has roots, however, in a more subtle and important aspect of humanity: understanding how people solve problems.

People solve countless problems throughout the day. A problem need not be something as formal as a math equation. Consider the increasingly common problem of understanding how to use a cell phone to make a phone call. Understanding the various buttons, navigating the menus, and ultimately placing the call is a problem to be solved, and a method to understand how people approach problems of this kind would be of huge value to anyone in the business of shaping complicated user experiences.

Herb Simon, arguably the father of the field of artificial intelligence and a beautiful thinker, was also interested in how people solved problems, yet his goal was a bit more lofty than creating a cell phone. In order to create intelligent computer systems that may simulate or predict human behavior, one must first understand how human behavior itself works. Simon, along with Allen Newell, developed a series of experiments to understand issues of cognition and working and long-term memory. [32] Through these experiments, Newell and Simon determined that, among other things, people could articulate what they were doing, as they did it, without affecting the outcome of the task. That is, a person can attempt to dial a cell phone and explain *what* he is doing, as long as he is not prompted to explain *why* he is doing it. This running description of action—formally called a protocol—is, ultimately, an intimate look at the contents of the working memory in a participant. Evaluators can use this technique to understand what someone is doing, and can later interpret why that person did it. By understanding what people have done, designers can begin to understand when they have errors and can interpret, or create credible stories about these errors. Additionally, designers can understand the rationale behind actions by seeing them in totality. Actions will appear as a running set of steps in a task to achieve a goal. The protocol can be interpreted by designers, who can then contemplate the underlying behavior that occurred.

In order to successfully conduct a Think Aloud User Study, a designer requires a prototype, a participant, and a set of tasks. A prototype is a representation of the final product. The prototype can be of any fidelity.

32 Herb Simon and Allen Newell are responsible for a number of advances in the fields of computer science and cognitive psychology, and can continually be found throughout the literature relating to Interaction Design and Human Computer Interaction. Newell worked with Stuart Card and Tom Moran in developing a unified vision of human-computer interaction when the field was still in its infancy, and ultimately co-authored the text *The Psychology of Human-Computer Interaction*. He helped build the computing system and computer science department at Carnegie Mellon University. Simon's list of accomplishments is no less impressive, and includes the ACM A.M. Turing Award in 1975 with Allen Newell and the Nobel Prize in Economics in 1978. Newell and Simon are continually recognized with the Newell-Simon Hall at Carnegie Mellon University, which houses, among other things, the Human-Computer Interaction Institute.

For example, if testing a piece of software, the prototype can either be a functioning and working version of the software or a simple set of hand-drawn screens. When testing physical products, the level of finish given to the testable model is relative to the complexity of a task.

Just as the prototype should be representative of the final design, so should the participant represent the end users of the creation. For example, when testing products intended for use in an industrial kitchen, it is worthwhile to find participants who spend a great deal of time in industrial kitchens and actually represent the target audience of the product. One way of approximating end users is to attempt to locate individuals who are similar to the Personas that have been previously developed.

A set of tasks will be given to the participant. These tasks attempt to engage the participant in actions that represent normal behavior when using a product, and should thus be structured around predictable and probable goals a user may have. Referencing the previously developed Personas and Scenarios makes sense when developing tasks for the Think Aloud User Study.

Once the prototype has been created, the participant has been recruited and the tasks have been established, running the study is straightforward. It is, in fact, so simple that it may seem too easy. The difficulty is not in the mechanics of the procedure, but in the interpretation and application of the results. The prototype is presented to the participant, and he is instructed to use it to accomplish the tasks. He is then asked to "think out loud" as he uses the prototype: He is to vocalize what he is doing throughout the task. If he falls silent, the facilitator will prompt him to continue talking, but will be unable to help him in any way. These instructions frequently become comical as participants realize that they

are, truly, on their own. Once the rules for the study are established, and a sample "think out loud" is demonstrated, participants generally take to the technique quickly and only a little prompting is required to keep them continually verbal.

Less formal but still useful versions of the technique have evolved that focus more on moderator-led probing and less on simple vocalization of working memory. Moderators may ask questions like "Is that what you expected to happen?" or "You look confused—is there something on the screen that isn't what you expected?" in an effort to draw out reactions from participants. The value of any form of user testing is in the critical incidents that are recorded during the protocol: "By an incident is meant any observable human activity that is sufficiently complete in itself to permit inferences and predictions to be made about the person performing the act… To be critical, an incident must occur in a situation where the purpose or intent of the act seems fairly clear to the observer and where its consequences are sufficiently definite to leave little doubt concerning its effects." [33] These incidents usually indicate design errors relating to navigation, cognitive structure, or labeling, and can be wonderful insights into the way people approach problems relating to designed interfaces and objects.

Perhaps even of more value than uncovering usability problems, however, is the direct manner in which these usability problems can be communicated to individuals in a position to effect positive change. Video of the user testing can be shown to engineers, project or product managers, marketers, or others involved in the development of a product. The

33 Flanagan, John. "The Critical Incident Technique." *Psychological Bulletin*, 51 (4), 1954. p327-358.

reactions of *real people* serve to appropriately contextualize the designs that have been created. Rather than having debate or discussion about what *could* happen, this type of user study presents something that *did* happen.

A thoughtful reflection of the process

The final step in the Interaction Process proposed by Zimmerman, Evenson, and Forlizzi focuses on Reflection—the act of assessing success. "Design researchers can examine their own process throughout the case and identify opportunities for increasing efficiency. Also, through the collection of reflections and summaries of many case studies, designers can begin to develop models that allow them to more accurately estimate both the time and resources needed for future projects."[34]

Unfortunately, this critical step is nearly always ignored by professional designers. Assessment implies internal criticism, something many companies prefer to leave up to public relations or external product reviews. The assessment must be at a user and project level, rather than a quality assurance level, and benchmarks for success have generally not been developed or acknowledged within corporate America. In many high-pressure design consultancies, to reflect means to waste time. Reflection is not productive, and is frequently viewed as a poor use of money and resources.

The process described above is very succinct and appears to be quite linear. In fact, process is elusive and messy, and a cohesive process frequently means a process of relative "unawareness" of structure. That is, there is rarely a definitive declaration of "beginning" or "ending" to any of the steps mentioned. Design is a creative field, and in order to successfully create, one must achieve a sense of Flow.[35] Flow is, among other things, the absence of self-doubt and the nearly auto-telic and automatic creative process. Beginning students of design are painfully aware of their process. They reflect, and doubt, and self-criticize both their creations and their skills. They are like the gawky thirteen-year-old girl who has sprouted up too quickly, nearly a head taller than the rest of the kids and obviously slouching to fit in. To be so painfully aware of "deficiencies" causes others to notice and comment on these shortcomings as well. Malcolm Gladwell discusses the fragility of process in his text *Blink*, making the connection between the creative process (flow) and the sports process (in the zone): "…problems that require a flash of insight operate by different rules… as human beings, we are capable of extraordinary leaps of insight and instinct… all these abilities are incredibly fragile. Insight is not a light bulb that goes off inside our heads. It is a flickering candle that can easily be snuffed out."[36] A mature designer respects and embraces the often ill-structured nature of the process, and—because he knows to expect

34 Zimmerman, John., Forlizzi, Jodi, and Evenson, Shelley. "Taxonomy for Extracting Design Knowledge from Research Conducted During Design Cases." Futureground 2004 (Conference of the Design Research Society) Proceedings, Melbourne, Australia, November 2004.

35 Csikszentmihalyi, Mihaly. *Creativity : Flow and the Psychology of Discovery and Invention.* Harper Perennial, 1996.

36 Gladwell, Malcolm. *Blink : The Power of Thinking Without Thinking.* Little, Brown, 2005. p122.

messiness during the act of creation—he promptly forgets about it completely. Process becomes innate, and the phenomenon of design intuition takes over.

The role of intuition

Design intuition is most likely not a genetic disposition to be creative. In the same way that one is not "predisposed" to be a doctor, or a lawyer, a designer must ultimately select a career path and hone the particular skills necessary to succeed in that path through a great deal of practice. What many refer to as "intuition," then, is not the untaught or un-teachable, but instead, is a learned understanding and respect of process, molded by experience and refined over a great deal of time and practice. Designers may appear to work based on "intuition," but the magical nature of an innate process carries little weight among engineers or business owners. Designers have learned to externalize and justify the above process along the way, in an effort to alleviate the pain that may come from explaining how a design "just feels right."

A designer who trusts his intuition does not abandon the procedural set of pragmatic steps as outlined above. Instead, he learns to balance this process with two outside forces: confidence, and personal experience. Confidence allows the designer to form an opinion *and then believe in it*. This confidence is informed by personal experiences, experiences that rarely have anything to do with the subject matter of a given design problem. Philippe Starck, a French designer who has found his way into popular retail stores and thus into the lives of many Americans, has been one of the most vocal proponents of "intuitive design." His confidence is obvious in the dramatic, and often amusing, style of his work—and the experiences from which he seems to draw have nothing to do with design, proper and instead frequently pertain to sex or the erotic nature of the human form.

Starck explains that as a designer, you "must have your own responsibility, your own consciousness... I work only with intuition."[37] It is interesting, then, to see the highly charged results of such an intuitive approach—Starck lives passionately, feels passionately, and has thus been continually described as a "sellout" or a "playboy." He may well be both things, but the dramatic success of his products at Target imply a sense of resonant emotional wonder with the audiences he is trying to reach.

Not all of the well-known and successful, or "high-profile" designers have embraced intuition in the process of design. Stefano Marzano, CEO and Chief Creative Director at Philips Design, has vocalized a near polar-opposite view of the role of designer. While Starck explains that "... there are already thousands of really, really good chairs. There are thousands of good lamps. There are thousands of everything... I am not interested in designers," Marzano takes a much more refined and intellectual approach, and views a process-driven design methodology as a business differentia- tor.[38] During a profound speech to the German Marketing Association Conference in Hamburg, Marzano explained that "... 'arty' product design, the sort of strikingly individual designs produced by Philippe Starck... may help provide differentiation for a while, but it is easily imitated and soon becomes a commodity." Instead of relying on the artistic intuitive, Philips practices a user-centered design process that relies on researching "social, cultural and visual trends by various international institutes and universities" in order to help shape complicated experiences.[39]

One can ultimately consider the outspoken artist of Starck and the humble and subdued intellect of Marzano as having the same positive focus: a focus on people, and emotions, and on making the world a better place to live in. This may embrace the visual aesthetic and lead to the production of objects of visual beauty, or focus on the creation of products that save lives and increase the value of the human condition. Both de- signers, however, view the role of design as a human-centered, emotionally driven, complicated, and culturally relevant process of creation.

The role of Design in the business process

During the process of Design, various disciplines claim ownership at various times. In some larger companies, Designers frequently complain of the "over the wall" problem. Research is conducted by Marketing, and

Mouse, designed by Philippe Starck.

37 Starck, Philippe. Lecture at Harvard University Graduate School of Design: Design Arts Initiative Lectures. October, 1997.

38 Designboom. Interview with Philippe Starck. May 23, 2005. <http://www.designboom.com/eng/interview/starck.html>

39 Marzano, Stefano. Lecture at the German Marketing Association Conference. November 9, 2004.

"thrown over the wall" to the Engineers. The Engineers build to the written specification, and over the wall it goes to the Designers. The Designers are left to do the plastics or push the pixels, and there is little communication or cohesion between disciplinary entities.

Philippe Starck designs a product as an individual, and while his products are sold in large companies like Target, his specific design consultancy is small. As a result, Starck generally enjoys making executive decisions spanning across design, marketing, engineering, and distribution. A designer at the larger entity of Philips, however, may be much more constrained to specific actions and may not have any input into issues tangentially related to design. In a development team made up of engineering, marketing, and design, each participant has a distinct role to play and the relationship forged by the various disciplines helps determine the relative success of the product.

The engineer may be responsible for the functionality of the product, and in the case of digital or electronic products, that functionality is frequently embedded in emerging technology. The engineer implicitly becomes the *advocate for technology*. While not necessarily proposing the latest technological advancements, the engineer remains responsible for making sure that a product is technically sound and that it functions correctly. Similarly, a marketing manager may be responsible for ensuring that a brand presents a consistent and compelling image. This may include understanding the target demographic as well as gaining an awareness of purchasing patterns and buying trends. A project manager may own the product development schedule, and be responsible for delivering the project as specified, on time and on budget. Each player in the development of a product has a primary focus.

The Interaction Designer, too, takes ownership of a particular area of expertise. While engineers may be advocates for *function*, and marketers for *brand*, the Interaction Designer becomes an advocate for *humanity*. This advocacy must occur on various levels of detail as a project progresses from a business goal into a tangible form.

At the beginning stages of a project, an idea may be driven solely by a business necessity: increasing profits, gaining brand equity, or disrupting a traditional channel leader. The Interaction Designer, if invited to discuss the project at this stage, may ask questions like "Does the user need this product at all?" This view might be informed by an understanding of culture, or an intricate care and love of society. It may, however, simply be a representation of viewing the world through a technologically-wary filter. This is, clearly, a philosophical question first; the "right" answer may be the "wrong" business suggestion, and Interaction Designers are rarely invited to discuss the project at this stage. This is unfortunate. If the process of Interaction Design is to be applied to the business processes themselves, Designers need to be firmly embedded in the upper echelons of the corporation, or have a strong relationship with those upper levels of management.

Further along in the process of product development, it may become apparent that particular elements of functionality are more difficult or expensive to implement. At this stage in the project, the Interaction Designer is responsible for forcing a dialogue of cost/benefit analysis from the perspective of the end user. How much contextual evidence is there for such an element of functionality? What is the value of a more expensive piece of technology, measured on a human scale, rather than a financial scale?

As a project nears completion, Interaction Designers are frequently called upon to consider the visual aesthetics of a solution. This detailed level of refinement gives the Interaction Designer a final chance to advocate for the end user—this time, on a purely emotional, or visual, level. In this way, *Interaction* Design often becomes synonymous with *Interactive* Design or *Graphical User Interface* (GUI) Design.

Interactive Design focuses on the development of interactive systems, placing technology at the center of attention and ultimately emphasizing authoring techniques. These authoring techniques frequently focus on the visual aesthetic of content presentation—the "eye candy" relating to interfaces. GUI Design takes a similar approach, emphasizing the nature of technological constraints and platform-specific paradigms. While these two disciplines certainly cater towards a user, they place a dramatic degree of emphasis on technology, and allow technical constraints to guide the development of interfaces. An Interaction Designer will most likely have skills related to Interactive Design or GUI Design, but these skills do not define his existence.

At the core of an interaction is the dialogue between a product, system, or service—and a person. Design exists as a means to a greater end—enhancing the human experience, solving complicated problems, and ultimately creating designs that resonate with their audience. Understanding that design work has direct consequences on people adds a unique, and humane, side to the elements present in the act of creation and dramatically shifts the focus of what could otherwise be thought of as technical artwork. At the heart of the Interaction Design process is a simple notion: that design should be user-centered, and that the only way to truly understand what users want is to interact with them. The process described attempts to capture what people do, think, say, and want so that a designer can create usable, useful, and desirable creations.

CHAPTER FOUR:
MANAGING COMPLEXITY

During the process of design, the Interaction Designer attempts to construct meaningful visualizations between individual components in an effort to understand hidden relationships. The ultimate goal of the creation of these visualizations is to understand. By reframing ideas in new and interesting ways, the designer can gain a deeper understanding of the abstract and semantic connections between ideas. These visualizations can then be used to communicate to other members of a design team, or can be used as platforms for the creation of generative sketching or model making. Frequently, the act of diagramming is a form of synthesis, and is a way to actively gain knowledge.

Structuring data in order to make useful information

Many Interaction Designers find themselves simultaneously filling two roles: Interaction Designer and Information Architect. The subfield of Information Architecture has gained recognition primarily as a web development discipline, usually associated with mapping out and understanding the connections within large, complicated websites. The discipline and techniques also shape the underlying structure of proper Interaction Design, as the Information Architecture techniques seems to illustrate how a successful Interaction Designer approaches any design problem at all (regardless of medium or intended outcome).

Author Richard Saul Wurman is responsible for coining the phrase Information Architecture in 1975. His background, in the traditional field of Architecture, supports his interest in way finding and navigation. The world of Information Architecture can be thought of as a discipline of map making, but maps need not be related only to geography. People use a map to find their way, and they need to find their way whenever they are lost. Sometimes, however, maps are used in an exploratory manner, simply to discover what is unknown. Clearly, the level of complexity of modern and futuristic products and systems will disorient a great number of people. By understanding—and visualizing—connections between elements and seemingly unrelated systems, the Interaction Designer can provide the common trail toward understanding.

One of the largest and most documented usability issues evident within the structure of the World Wide Web concerns navigation. Specifically, people don't truly understand where they are, where they have been, and where they are going as they traverse the Internet. Nor should they, as the concept of placement within a virtual system is truly foreign, and no matter the metaphor provided, most people don't really understand—or have time to understand—the essence of computing across a large, distributed network. The vastness of the structure of the Internet is simply too large for many people to actually consider. The conceptual undertaking of visualizing something that has no immediate physical manifestation is a difficult task to engage in. While the World Wide Web is an obvious example of this sort of limitless environment, the same general location-based confusion is evident in the menu systems of smaller handheld devices, such as digital cameras and telephones, and in embedded systems in vehicles (intended—ironically—to aid in physical navigation).

Alan Cooper discusses the issue with relationship to permanent objects, or reference points:

> "One of the most important aids to navigation is a simple interface without a lot of places to navigate to. By places, I mean modes, forms and major dialogues. Beyond reducing the number of navigable places, the only way to enhance the user's ability to find his way around in

the program is by providing better points of reference. In the same way that sailors navigate by reference to shorelines or stars, users navigate by reference to permanent objects placed in the program's user interface."[40]

Authors Peter Morville and Louis Rosenfeld agree in their text *Information Architecture*, but acknowledge that this is easier said than done:

> "Many contextual clues in the physical world do not exist on the Web. There are no natural landmarks and no north or south. Unlike physical travel, hypertextual navigation allows users to be transported right into the middle of a large unfamiliar web site. Links from remote web pages and search engine result pages allow users to completely bypass the front door or main page of the web site."[41]

Design literature frequently mentions a four-step process taken as individuals gain comprehension. This comprehension could be an understanding of digital-spatial relationships in a complicated system, or the awareness of how to achieve a goal. This four-step process attempts to move from Data to Information, to Knowledge, and finally to Wisdom (DIKW). The path has been routinely analyzed in fields of Information Technology and Knowledge Management, and is mentioned by designer Nathan Shedroff in a brief article titled "An Overview of Understanding."[42]

40 Cooper, Alan. *About Face: The Essentials of User Interface Design.* John Wiley & Sons, 1995. p508.

41 Morville, Peter, and Louis Rosenfeld. *Information Architecture for the World Wide Web: Designing Large-Scale Web Sites.* Copyright © 2006, 2002, 1998 O'Reilly Media, Inc. Used with permission. All rights reserved. p50.

42 Shedroff, Nathan. "An Overview to Understanding" in *Information Anxiety* 2, p27.

Interaction Designers can think of this DIKW path as a framework for progressive learning. One goal of design may be to assist people through this path as they use designed creations.

Data alone has little value. Although "data" usually implies numbers, it simply represents discrete units of content. This content may be factual or opinion driven, and it may be useful or useless. Creating information out of data may seem a simple task, then: Present to the user the units of data that are relevant and remove the rest. What, though, would be deemed relevant in, say, a painting? Are the marks on the canvas relevant bits of data? What about the absence of marks—the "whitespace"? Or the implied marks, found in the gesture of the applied paint? Making information out of data, a seemingly easy task, is quickly confounded when the designer attempts to integrate elements of aesthetics or emotion.

Information can be thought of as meaningful data. This is usually created "by design"—using the creative process to bring together elements and to form relationships that, perhaps, were previously hidden among the "irrelevant data." To know that it is raining in Pittsburgh is data. To understand that it has been raining in Pittsburgh for the past week and you are visiting the Steel City tomorrow is informative: You had better pack your raincoat. Information is the organization of data in ways that illustrate meaning. This organization may, in fact, alter the meaning itself. This has an important implication, as the meaning of seemingly objective data is altered by the appearance and structure of that data.

If information is meaningful data, knowledge, then, is a result of the combination of elements of information in order to arrive at a principle, a theory, or a story. While information may be sensory, knowledge seems to be more complicated, and perhaps more experience-driven. Storytelling has a long history as a mechanism of knowledge transfer, and can be considered a rapid immersion in experience: One cannot *experience* time travel, but one can gain knowledge about the act of time travel through a rich, compelling, and highly experiential story. This idea of knowledge as extended dialogue is highly relevant when considered in the guise of experience and Interaction Design. The design of behavior may, in fact, be the design of action-based knowledge (telling a story through motion).

Wisdom, often thought of as enlightenment, can result from applying knowledge in a new and novel manner. There is wisdom to be found in emotion—in happiness and pain—and even the youngest designer can apply knowledge and emotion in new ways, given the opportunity.

This path from Data to Wisdom may be the underlying goal of all Information Architecture activities. The acquisition of Knowledge obviously occurs over time, and this is where the Interaction Designer excels. Behavior occurs in the fourth dimension, and Interaction Design techniques attempt to understand and, hopefully, shape the way people act over time.

Designing with the fourth dimension in mind

Traditional designers of artifacts—Graphic Designers, or Industrial Designers—typically view the relationships between a product and a person in a very finite sense. A user may interact with a toaster through a discrete set of actions (place toast in toaster, set brownness level, press toast down, wait for toast to pop up, remove toast), and the designer is responsible for creating a product that affords, or encourages, all of these activities. This view of affordance implies ease of use and clarity of task. It needs to be apparent to a user that he has a certain role to play, and if he plays it correctly, he will have a nice breakfast.

While this view is useful for the design of simple and relatively mundane objects, it simply doesn't work for the creation of complicated interfaces that "live" for an extended period of time. Consider the length of an engagement between a person and a Microsoft Outlook Inbox. When first acknowledged (or "installed), Microsoft Outlook is very exacting. Every installation of Outlook will be the same; the toolbars will be in the same place, each element will behave in the same way, and the system is very predictable. If the system is predictable, the dialogue between the system and the user is also fairly predictable. Designers can guess, with a fair degree of accuracy, what will happen. At the very best, this guessing can be substantiated: Designers can, during the creation of this project, do a bit of contextual research and actually *watch* people go about using a prototype of Microsoft Outlook.

This accuracy quickly diminishes as *real life* takes over. People set up mail accounts. They receive and respond to mail. They use Outlook to organize their life, rather than to simply organize their mail. They make errors, and customize palettes, and change color schemes. And over time, Microsoft Outlook becomes a very different product from the original installation. It is very difficult to "model" what might occur even a week past the initial installation of this software, as the complexity of real life makes for an exponential curve of change. Nonetheless, the Interaction Designer may indeed be asked to find a way to model this complicated scenario. This fourth-dimensional pattern of use—understanding how time plays a role in the use of a product—begins to clearly articulate the distinctions between two similarly named and commonly confused activities: User Interface Design and Interaction Design. Both activities are usually performed by the same person, but with dramatically different purposes.

A designer focusing on the User Interface (UI) or the Graphical User Interface (GUI) is generally not concerned with time as a defining characteristic in the use of a product. While he may consider the flow of use on a "page" (used loosely to illustrate one particular chunk of material being presented), and may even think of the flow of use from "page to page," he is not considering the long-term consequences of use at this stage in design. His focus is instead on widget placement, and button labeling, and pixel-level decisions of screen real estate. Sometimes, the rare software developer with a "visual eye" may take on the role of User Interface Designer. Additionally, User Interface Designers with a particular competency in development may take on the often ambiguous role of "User Interface *Developer,*" blurring the lines between design and implementation. The expert-blindspot rears its ugly head: Developers are, by definition, aware of technological constraints and will force their design to appease these constraints. While certainly a benefit to short development cycles, this technology-centric attitude will come at the expense of usability. The User Interface Developer will generally not consider conceptual solutions to the problem that, while more usable, may involve dramatic "back end" development changes.

The Interaction Designer shifts to attend to the detail and pragmatic details of UI design only after modeling or understanding the more conceptual behavior—activities or goals—that may drive the usage of a product. Several mapping and diagramming techniques exist to assist Interaction Designers in tracking product use over time. While referenced by various names in various disciplines, they all attempt to create systematic organization amidst complexity.

Using a concept map to understand relationship and vocabulary

A concept map is a visualization of present understanding of a system. It is intended to represent the mental model of a concept—to allow members of the development team to see the "forest and the trees." Generally, a concept map links nouns with verbs. It provides a visual way to understand relationships through literal connections as well as through proximity, size, shape, and scale. The tool is intended to illustrate relationships between entities. The act of creation is generative in the sense that the designer must make subjective value judgments on the strength of the relationships.

The first step towards creating a concept map is the creation of a concept matrix. This matrix lists all elements relevant to a particular domain (nouns) and attempts to identify which items have a direct relationship. Consider, for example, an analysis of the game of Baseball. One may identify nouns such as Ball, Bat, Umpire, Hot Dog, and Catcher as well as nearly one or two hundred other terms. By creating a matrix to illustrate the connections between these elements, the designer is forced to analyze the extent of the relationship. All of the words are implicitly related, as they all have to do with the overarching domain of Baseball. However, Ball is more closely related to Bat than it is to Hot Dog. By analyzing each and every term's connections to one another, the designer is forced to "zoom in" on the details to such an extent that he gains an intimate understanding of a discipline. He can then begin to understand the (sometimes obvious) hierarchy that exists within a large quantity of data. The elements with more relationships become the main branches on the concept map: They become the "glue" holding together the overarching discipline.

Once the matrix is created and these core concepts are identified, completing the concept map becomes a rather simple activity of connecting nouns with verbs. How are Ball and Bat related? The Ball is Hit with a Bat. How are Catcher and Ball related? The Catcher attempts to Catch the Ball. As these are added to the diagram, the designer—and eventually, the entire development team—can visually trace relationships between entities and understand how a potential change to one aspect of a system may ripple through the system as a whole.

Using a Process Flow Diagram to understand the logical flow of entities

Process Flow Diagrams are another visual form of organizing data into comprehensible systems. Also known as Data Flow Diagrams or Decision Tree Diagrams, these diagrams have traditionally been used in the fields of electrical engineering and in computer science to illustrate the logical flow of data through a system. These diagrams can be created relatively quickly, prior to implementing complicated systems, and then manipulated in order to understand the optimum flow of data. Interaction Designers use Process Flow Diagrams for a similar purpose. These diagrams assist in understanding the discrete rules, and their relationships to one another, that make up an activity. This analysis tool can then be shared with engineers in order to articulate and demonstrate the rationale behind design decisions. It can be used both as a generative exercise as well as an explanatory tool.

To create a Process Flow Diagram, an Interaction Designer first identifies, through various forms of ethnography, the operators in a system and their roles. These operators include many of the nouns as present in the Concept Map. Then, the "logic flow" is mapped out to connect the operators with actions. Take, for example, the phenomenon of a telephone ringing. The phone rings once and there is a clear path of available (and logical) repercussions to this ring. The caller may hang up, the telephone may be answered, or else the phone will ring again. This will happen several times in a row, at which time a new choice becomes available: The call may be answered by a voicemail system.

By creating a Process Flow Diagram, the designer has formed an intimate understanding of the possible logical outcomes of use with a system. While the diagram itself can be useful throughout the project, the act of creating the diagram is of much more importance. Those involved in the production of such a diagram have created a strong mental representation of the boundaries of a complicated system.

The classification of words

Both of the aforementioned diagrams embrace the visual over the textual. While they certainly include written words, the visual arrangement of the content creates an arguably more accessible way of examining a system or artifact. The diagrams rely on the use of words as placeholders for ideas, forms or artifacts. Language affects organization—and therefore,

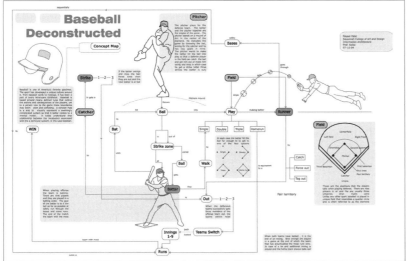

Concept Map of the game of Baseball. Payaal Patel.

usability—on a very pragmatic and immediate level. Categorization implies the method that is used to group elements within a larger context. People rely on language in design to encourage simplicity, yet language is often ambiguous and many designers are not adequately trained in the nuances the English language presents. Consider the implications of the common word, "cup." A cup is exactly two half cups, or four quarter cups; a cup of water weighs .521 pounds, and asking for a "cup of coffee" at Starbucks gives you offers of Tall, Grande, and Venti. Cup can be used as a verb ("He cupped his head in his hands"), or as a noun ("Put the cup in the sink"), and can refer to a commonplace drinking vessel, to the intimate inner workings of a piece of women's underwear, or to a hard piece of plastic that protects baseball players from unfortunate accidents. Designers, then, must understand the trivialities associated with the words they select for everything from the labels on a website to the packaging an object comes in.

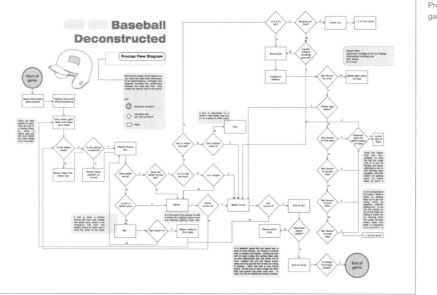

Process Flow Diagram of the game of Baseball. Payaal Patel.

Adobe product screen shot reprinted with permission from Adobe Systems Incorporated.

Adobe Illustrator®, one of the most widely used vector-based graphics programs, has often been analyzed in terms of its complexity and learning curve. Language adds a large degree of complexity to the program, as shown below.

The Type drop down menu presents common choices of Font and Size, but also more ambiguous elements like Glyphs, Threaded Text, Optical Margin Alignment, and Legacy Text. The Effect menu offers choices of Path and Pathfinder, *two* choices for Stylize, and the ability to "Sharpen Unsharp Mask." The complexity presented by the words puts the user in the difficult position of having to guess—and anticipate—what a function will do. Only when the feature has been committed to memory will these irrational labels make sense. To an expert, the label is simply a trigger to an already established pathway of understanding. But to a novice, these labels stand in the way of comprehension.

The Interaction Designer attempts to construct meaningful visualizations between individual components in an effort to understand hidden relationships. The ultimate goal of the creation of these visualizations is to understand; by reframing ideas in new and interesting ways, the designer can gain a deeper understanding of the abstract and semantic connections between ideas. This understanding can then be applied to the development of a system, service, or artifact.

A Mini Case Study: Tax Form Redesign

Even with the influx of digital communication devices, people still rely on old-fashioned, printed materials to get through their daily life. Poor information design can frustrate and disappoint a user, and often has a larger impact on their lives—people may miss meetings, appointments, or important events if they misjudge or misread a schedule or map. Designers of information-heavy systems need to understand and balance complicated data along with visual design principles to produce legible, comprehensible instruction materials.

Each year, every working adult in the United States must file his or her taxes, and while a number of people utilize online services for this task, millions of people still rely on the printed forms available from the Internal Revenue Service. In fact, in 2003, over 33 million individuals elected to self-prepare their 1040 forms by hand.[43] Students enrolled in a class called Information Architecture at the Savannah College of Art and Design were tasked with redesigning the 1040 United States Individual Income Tax Return form. The goals of the Tax Form Redesign project included conceptual as well as pragmatic outcomes. While an immediate goal was to make sense of complicated, domain-specific information, an implied goal was to understand the balance of visual and statistical data necessary to accurately inform a user.

....

43 The data comes from the IRS, and is even more interesting: 3 million people filed their taxes by telephone in 2003! The average refund was $2,010 and the IRS announced that over 92,000 refund checks were returned as undeliverable. In 2002, over $2 billion went uncollected in refunds.

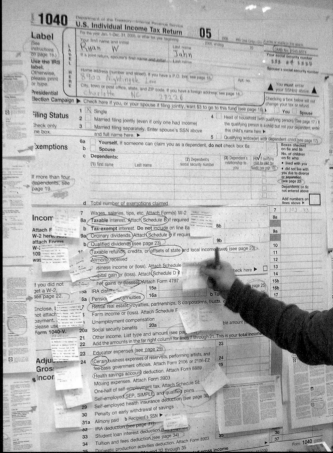

Using an iterative, user-centered design process, we have improved the experience of completing the 1040 tax form by restructuring the information in a way that promotes understanding and reinforces accuracy.

In order to redesign the form it is necessary to become a pseudo-expert in tax law and gain a firm grasp on the terminology related to the subject matter; this can be done through standard domain research. However, a much quicker way to establish an understanding is to perform contextual research. This method involves the understanding of work in its natural

highlighted problems in the existing forms and therefore shed light on potential solutions.

We feel strongly that visceral stimulations make users happy, which ultimately improves their problem-solving skills. This idea played a key role in the development of our redesign. The goal throughout the project was to keep the users visually stimulated, thereby engaging them in the process, and ultimately resulting in more accurately completed forms. Our concept went through several iterations; each round refined the form, as

Far left: Analysis of the existing tax form. Below: Users responding to the tax form.

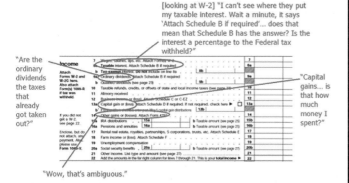

We moved from wireframe prototypes constructed on paper toward more developed computer models. At each phase in the project, we tested our iterations with real people to ensure that we were increasing usability and not negatively impacting the tax filing process.

The 1040 Individual Income Tax return form is targeted toward a vast mass of users; therefore, it includes a large number of variables—many of which are rarely used. The current form used by the IRS strives to include all the possible options. However, they are presented equally and in such a way that the user must collect information from multiple sources; in the end, they are left unsure of the initial goal. Users often rely on past experiences (sometimes simply copying the previous years' form entries) rather than reacting to the information that is provided by the form itself because they are overwhelmed by the densely packed data, unclear terminology and a poor navigation system.

Below and facing page: Four pages of a Tax Form Redesign.

Unlike the old form, our new form allows users with any level of understanding of the tax system to file their taxes. This is achieved by including explicit definitions of the main sections and allowing the users to understand the repercussions of their actions. Visual weight and new elements of aesthetics were added to direct attention. While users will still have to have a small grasp of concepts related to taxes, the new form makes it easier to determine where this information can be found.

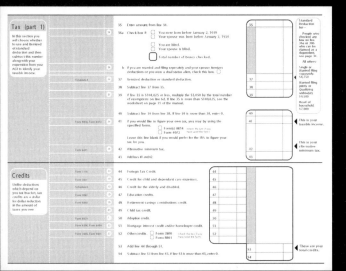

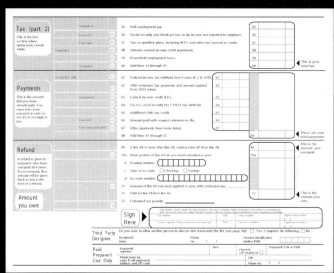

5

CHAPTER FIVE:
SHAPING AESTHETICS TO INFORM EXPERIENCE

Designers are in the unique position to improve all aspects of human life, including the visual, emotional, and experiential. Interaction Design should be desirable—beautiful, elegant, and appropriate—regardless of the medium chosen to visualize a solution. Visual form can be considered one of the most basic methods of communicating design solutions, and the associated field of Industrial Design has a relatively long period of formal development which can be directly applied to the creation of Interaction Design solutions.

While the roots of Industrial Design lie in the Industrial Revolution, the true essence of modern commercial design aesthetics can be traced to the styling exercises of vehicle designers in the 50s. Popularized by Raymond Loewy, the sleek, streamlined style of trains and cars can still be found in today's translucent plastic (and very fast looking) staplers, computer mice, and drinking bottles. Interaction Designers, however, are required to balance issues of form with issues of time: An interaction occurs in the fourth dimension, and simply attending to aesthetics does not take into account the unfolding experience that a user has with a product. Interaction Designers often find themselves in a position of imbalance between aesthetic appropriateness and the user-centeredness described above. Rhetorical issues of form development become increasingly important when considering solutions that embrace technology, as ambiguity of form may negatively impact understanding but may positively affect experience. Many Interaction Designers are deeply concerned with the nature of aesthetics, continually considering why objects look the way they do and analyzing the relationship between particular cultural movements, brand identity "formulas," and trends. Several of these trends are rooted in nature, while others are reactionary to issues of mechanization or mass production. The following articulate, briefly, several relationships or trends that can be found in the design and development of objects.

Aesthetic relationships between nature and technology

Biomimicry, or Bionics, attempts to study nature and then imitate it or take inspiration from it in the creation of new products and systems. The natural world has evolved slowly and methodically, and it seems appropriate to look to it for inspiration in both form as well as solutions to problems. The typically referenced example of Biomimicry as applied to problem solving can be seen when comparing burrs growing on a plant with an innovative

product development: Velcro. The hook and loop-style attachment that allows cockleburs to stick to animals is, in essence, the same method that allows Velcro to close and stay closed. Proponents of Biomimicry look to the natural world for inspiration in form development. For example, Yoon Ho Choi, a designer at Motorola, designed the PEBL telephone to be a simple form that was reminiscent of a river rock. It is interesting to note that there are very few, if any, symmetrical and rectilinear objects in nature. Much of nature is oblong and amorphous, and while plants, trees, and animals all have a sense of balance, they are not "perfect" as is usually the case with mass-produced objects. In an effort to encourage a poetic aesthetic related to Biomimicry, designers sometimes reference this subtle hint of error—much like an artist or craftsman may purposely introduce elements to illustrate the individual nature of his creations.[44]

Similar to Biomimicry in its reference to nature, Anthropomorphism can be thought of as the psychological process of assigning real-life (often human or animalistic) qualities to inanimate objects: essentially, Anthropomorphism is the process of personification. These forms frequently personify human sexuality, as found in a number of Allessi products. The idea of a "phallic symbol" is often alluded to when considering long and thin consumer electronics such as electric toothbrushes or umbrella handles, and has even been referenced with regard to the new Freedom Tower planned for the site of the old World Trade Center towers. The allusion need not be sexual, however. Designer Alessandro Mendini can be thought of as a proponent of Anthropomorphism in a more childlike way, as he envisions fantastic imaginative characters and his designs clearly reference human and animal forms. The results are accessible, friendly, and fairly whimsical designs. The products beg to be handled, and speak a clear and refined, albeit childlike, language.

In contrast to Biomimicry and Anthropomorphism, the Industrialization style seems to make vivid formal reference to the Industrial Revolution—to mechanics, pneumatics, and the technical advancement that is made possible by machinery and mass production. Through a Designer's choice of materials, as well as formal qualities, a product can seem more technically "advanced" than it actually is. Consider the perforated aluminum metal on the chassis of the Apple Power Mac G5 tower. Arguably, these holes serve no functional purpose with regard to heat dissipation, and offer instead a dramatic aesthetic value. They make the tower look as if it is a technically powerful machine. The punched metal offers an aggressive feel that alludes to the force of the act of creation—violent, but only subtly. It is curious that Apple, a company considered to be progressively in favor of advocating for humanity, would choose such an inhumane look and feel for its products. This Industrialized look is subtly present in Windows applications, as the default User Interface commonly has beveled gray edges and a gradient of gray tones. David Gelernter has deemed this quality "machine beauty," alluding to the harmony that occurs in a mechanized environment, as a connection is formed between human and machine.[45] Associated with this notion of Industrialization is the phenomenon of Streamlining,

44 There is an interesting anecdote about Amish woman purposely adding errors to their quilts, as only God could make a perfect quilt. These errors, known as "humility blocks," create a sense of uniqueness in each creation. The very humane and romantic idea, however, doesn't pan out. Bettina Havig, an author and an avid quilter, explains that if you "Ask an Amish quilter about the 'humility block'… the answer will be 'I make enough mistakes without making them on purpose.'"

45 Gelernter, David. *Machine Beauty: Elegance and the Heart of Technology*. New York, NY: Basic Books, 1998.

which literally involves shaping an object to reduce the amount of drag or resistance to motion as the object moves through a stream of air. This is clearly important in aircraft design, as the goal tends toward efficiency and speed. One may question the importance of a "fast pencil sharpener," yet when viewed in relation to the political and economic situation in America at the time of creation, Raymond Loewy's 1933 design hints at a future of potential—of excess and speed, but with a human, and human amorphousness.

A rejection of all of the above styling techniques is the notion of minimalism in visual form. "Omit the unimportant in order to emphasize the important[46]," declares Dieter Rams, the former Head of Product Design and Executive Director at Braun. Rams rebels against the aggression of extraneous decoration and what he called "destructive, aggressive tendencies." When considered as dialogue, these extraneous elements convolute the message. The disconnect between designer and audience is enhanced by the noise of artificial stimuli. For Rams, less is more. Another Dieter Rams meme is that "good design is as little design as possible." The notion of minimalism has been adopted as the modern aesthetic of choice in posh New York apartments, where the trend is embodied in much modern architecture and internal furnishings. The execution of minimalism is particularly difficult, as the less there is, the more it matters.

Visual form language creates product families

Each of these styles are ways of thinking about groups of products in a static setting—a single product, and a single moment in time. A more useful way of grouping products based on form language has to do with a brand language of *experience*. Products, both physical and digital, rarely exist on their own—a sole coffee maker, or a single piece of software—and they rarely exist in an idle state. Instead, products exist in families, groups of several products or product lines, and are used over time. A product family can be as robust as a dining room furniture set, or as intricately detailed as various types of wine glasses. Product families are almost entirely defined by, and generally succeed because of their visual language. Common visual form and language can even create a visual family within an entire brand. Braun products are defined by their stark, simple, and exacting form, while Oxo products are identifiable by their large, comfortable qualities and their comforting materials. Consider the Volkswagen product family. While the Jetta is a substantially different vehicle from the Beetle, both appear to belong in the same family. This is made even clearer when both of these vehicles are placed next to a Chevrolet Suburban. The curves and bubbly "puffed up" nature of the Volkswagen becomes incredibly clear when viewed next to the hard, boxy, and plain lines of the Chevy. This is due to the sum of the formal characteristics, details and functions, and transitions and intersections embodied in the vehicles' exteriors. These elements have all been purposely shaped to indicate a particular brand language. Both software and hardware companies alike frequently have a strict style guide that indicates the aesthetic qualities allowed in their

46   Rams, Dieter. "Omit the Unimportant." *Design Discourse: History, Theory, Criticism.* Ed Victor Margolin. The University of Chicago Press, 1989. p111.

products. Interaction Designers work with (or as) graphic or visual designers to establish consistent sizes, placements, shapes, colors, and styles in order to continually reinforce brand language.

The role of brand in visual families

In the past decade, brand experience has been recognized as a substantial and critical component to the world of product development. The rise of the mega-brands Starbucks and Nike has created a new set of "rules" for marketers. It is no longer necessary to spend each dollar of a marketing budget on the sale of product. Instead, large amounts of money are spent on raising brand awareness or gaining "mind share." Issues of placement, messaging, stickiness, and experience are all marketing terms that have crept into discussions of product design and even into the design of interactive multimedia. Julie Khaslavsky and Nathan Shedroff have discussed the role brand plays in what they have deemed the "Seductive Experience": "Ending a seduction successfully is like parting from a romantic relationship on good terms. It should always be viewed as a positive, worthwhile experience—if the creator of the product wants a chance at seducing the same customers again or being held in high regard for having created the experience in the first place."[47] Scott Bedbury, author of *A New Brand World* (and creator of such memorable brand campaigns as Nike's *Just*

---

47 Khaslavsky, Julie, and Nathan Shedroff. "Understanding the Seductive Experience" in *Communications of the ACM*, May 1999, Vol 42. No 5. p49. Association for Computing Machinery, Inc. Reprinted by permission.

Do It) claims several principles to understand and develop this seductive brand awareness. Not surprisingly, he concludes that "Relevance, simplicity, and humanity—not technology—will distinguish brands in the future."[48]

Recall the last time you enjoyed a cup of coffee at Starbucks. The store probably welcomed you with soft, subdued lighting; the warm and rich colors on the wall set a backdrop for the array of comfortable, over-sized chairs and couches that surround the perimeter of the store. Before the barista welcomed you with a smile, the music playing complemented the physical with soft and often jazz-inspired rhythms. All of this, however, is trivialized by the rich and delightful scents of freshly brewed coffee and rich pastries.

As you approached the counter, you may not have noticed, and you certainly may not like, that you were being carefully manipulated to feel—and even behave—in a certain way: in the Starbucks Way. The colors, scents, process, procedures, placement, artifacts, heights, weights, materials, curves, transitions, forms, tastes, and products are all carefully orchestrated to ensure that you have a successful experience during your stay at Starbucks. A major theme of this experience is comfortable predictability, as the experience at a Starbucks in Portland, Oregon, is nearly identical to the experience at a Starbucks in New York City. The brand of Starbucks has transcended the simple mark or logo that is usually referenced to delineate a particular company. If prompted, you may even be hard-pressed to describe the logo itself. Instead, when you next purchase a tub of Starbucks Ice Cream at the corner grocery store, you will recall the feeling you had when you last enjoyed a Venti Half Caff Latte with a Biscotti.

Starbucks Corporation is not selling coffee, as much as they are selling an experience. When considering the actual product that is being consumed, the coffee begins to play a rather inconsequential role. In fact, Starbucks intends to become your "home away from home." The 2004 Starbucks Annual Report explains that the corporation has the goal of becoming a third place for people to go—instead of home or work—where they can feel comfortable and, more important, loyal. [49] And it is not rare for a company to consider their business as a "third place to go." Gap, Inc.'s Forth & Towne stores intended to create a welcoming place for middle-aged women to relax and unwind,[50] and Apple has also made an effort to sell experience: "One thing completely obscured from view as you enter the store: the cash registers. It feels more like walking into a hands-on museum than walking into a retail store. Sure, Apple wants to sell products, but their first priority is to make you want the products. And that desire has to begin with your experience of the products in the store."[51]

Starbucks also understands the importance of the seductive experience in generating return business. After creating the framework for a compelling and predictable experience, the product itself—coffee—is consistently top quality and unique, communicating the message that Starbucks is focused on the highest standard of excellence. This is communicated in totality, through happy employees (or "partners", who are

48 Bedbury, Scott. *A New Brand World : Eight Principles for Achieving Brand Leadership in the Twenty-First Century*. Penguin, 2003. p183

49 Starbucks 2004 Annual Report, p13.

50 "It Sure Ain't Old Navy." *Businessweek*. October 17, 2005.
<http://www.businessweek.com/magazine/content/05_42/b3955100.htm>

51 Garrett, Jesse James. "Six Design Lessons from the Apple Store." July 9th, 2004.
<http://www.adaptivepath.com/publications/essays/archives/000331.php>

eligible for such impressive benefits as a 401K plan for part-timers and full health insurance) and through total immersion of the Starbucks experience in the United States.

Designers at Starbucks, Forth & Towne, and Apple have explored the nature of experience and the role it plays in the creation of sales—they have focused their efforts on the shopping experience. The designed product is ambiguous, and it becomes difficult to understand the relationship between physical and formal qualities of a product, and the experience in which it is bought, used, or discarded. In fact, this distinction may be irrelevant. Interaction Designers do not consider a designed artifact as distinct from the experience in which is it found.

Moving from artifacts to experiences

Dr. Kees Overbeeke, an associate professor of Industrial Design at TU/Eindhoven, describes this meshing of object and experience in his text "Tangible Products: Redressing the Balance Between Appearance and Action":

> "In our work, we see design for usability and design for aesthetics of interaction as inextricably linked. Much of the Interaction Design community reasons from usability towards aesthetics: poor usability may have a negative impact on the beauty of interaction. This has led to a design process in which usability problems are tackled first and questions about aesthetics are asked later. Yet, we are also interested in reasoning in the other direction: working from aesthetics and using

it to improve usability. We consider temptation to form part of an invitation for action, both through aesthetics of appearance and the prospect of aesthetics of interaction."[52]

As aesthetics and experience are so closely related, it is important to evaluate not only the emotional or experiential resonance in the creations, but also to understand or contemplate the structure of experiences with artifacts. The most succinct and oft-cited structure for understanding user experience was authored in 2000 by Jodi Forlizzi, of the Human-Computer Interaction Institute and School of Design at Carnegie Mellon, and Shannon Ford, formerly of Scient Corporation. Forlizzi and Ford identified the distinction between experience, an experience, and experience as story. *Experience* itself occurs (probably continually) during moments of consciousness, as to experience the world or to consider what is occurring in the world at a given moment. *An experience,* as discussed by John Dewey in *Art and Experience*, has a beginning, middle, and end. *Experience as story* is the vehicle used to transmit, condense, and reflect on an experience. The authors acknowledge that the creation of an experience is, most likely, impossible in and of itself, and that instead, designers are more fruitful in focusing their efforts on the creation of the structure in which an experience takes place:

> "We can realize that a good product is one that offers a good or memorable narrative that the user will engage with, and pass on to others, either by sharing the artifact or by talking about it. To create

---

52 Overbeeke, Kees, et al. "Tangible Products: Redressing the Balance Between Appearance and Action" in Pers Ubiquit Comput, Springer-Verlag London Limited, 2004. With kind permission of Springer Science and Business Media.

a good product, it is critical to understand our users. The need to involve the user in the design process has made product design a more complex task. However, designers can no longer focus solely on the product: a successful design will take into consideration all of the components in the user-product interaction: user, product, and context of use."[53]

Uday Gajendar, a designer, builds on the framework proposed by Forlizzi and Ford as he considers the role aesthetics and beauty play in the design of digital systems and devices. He too looks at the work of John Dewey as instrumental when considering experiences of aesthetic value, and explains that "A pleasurable emotional value derived from sensuous interaction may lead to a communication that speaks to one's central motive for life — perhaps related to what Joseph Campbell describes as the 'experience of being alive' — emotionally, spiritually, and culturally."[54] Gajendar concludes that "Interaction Designers should be concerned with the issue of beauty as our environment of experience becomes rapidly shaped by digital, networked, multifunctional artifacts that influence our lifestyles and perceptions."[55]

Designers are in the unique position to improve all aspects of human life, including the visual, emotional, and experiential. Interaction Design should be desirable—beautiful, elegant, and appropriate—regardless of the medium chosen to visualize a solution. And while the aesthetic refinement is important to the success of a product, the ability for that product to resonate in an experiential manner will allow that product to remain embedded in and positively affecting society and culture.

....

53 Forlizzi, Jodi, and Shannon Ford. "The Building Blocks of Experience: An Early Framework for Interaction Designers." DIS '00, Brooklyn, New York. Association for Computing Machinery, Inc. Reprinted by permission.

54 Gajendar, Uday. "Attention, Attraction, and the Aesthetic Value: Understanding Beauty as a Problem of User Experience" in *Designing Pleasurable Products and Interfaces*, 2003. Association for Computing Machinery, Inc. Reprinted by permission.

55 Ibid.

INTERACTION DESIGN AS BUSINESS LUBRICANT

Justin Petro, Thinktiv
Justin is currently the CEO of Thinktiv in Austin, Texas. Justin's previous experience includes retail and space design, industrial design, e-commerce, and user research. He's worked with clients such as Dell, Pricelock, Siemens, and Merrill Lynch and holds patents in hardware, software and retail design. Prior to founding Thinktiv, Justin worked as the Director of User Experience at Design Edge, HCI specialist for Trilogy Software, and Visual Interaction Designer at Maya Design Group. Justin holds a BFA from Carnegie Mellon University in Industrial Design.

We are at an impasse. Our profits are down; costs are up. We fight with our clients as much as we fight with ourselves. They don't listen to us, we don't listen to them, and we certainly don't listen to each other. We design new features rather than optimizing for specific needs; it is more and more common that marketing, not design, runs the show. Is there no end to this business cycle of commoditization? At the current rate, we are to be remembered as a bitter and disenchanted industry, a profession rewarded with paltry salaries for endless hours of pushing pixels and polishing radii. In case your bitter black turtle necked heart forgot for a moment, remember—as you dig in your tight jeans' pocket for enough change to get your double-mocha-skinny-latte fix: we are *designers*. We are agents for change.

Think back to the pre-internet era ten years ago, and relive the bubble ride again for a moment. Recall the promises we made to our clients, and how our profession began to shift: to embrace technology, and usability, and brand. We wanted to create something larger than a mark or product; we were after the customer experience. Can you remember what made us designers before the bubble burst? How quickly we forgot what made us special.

Do you remember the first time you got a book from Amazon or time shifted television on your Tivo? Our ability to think latterly, to diagnose problems, construct creative solutions, and think outside the proverbial Dell box is what makes us unique. These qualities are our saviors, not our handcuffs. It is our ability to think—not our ability to make—that we need to harness and embrace; further, it is our ability to think—not our ability to make—that should drive our compensation. It is time for a serious reinvention of our industry, ourselves, and what we call "business."

It's time for us to take back what is—and was—rightfully ours; the ability to create emotionally compelling solutions that our audience falls in love with. We have succumbed to a world where marketers "design," business people "research," and the bean counters run the show. We need to reclaim our role at the front end of our process; we have no business in the position we have relegated ourselves to: that of the implementer. We need to remember our oath as Designers and reclaim our role as strategist.

Tradition be damned

As designers, we are thinkers. While today's Designers come from myriad different backgrounds and educations and harbor diverse skill sets, we are still all the same: we are thinkers. In industry, we put up walls between ourselves and between our clients. We like to classify each other and characterize design as "industrial" or "graphic." But the discipline be damned: it is our ability to think creatively and broadly, not our physical output (be it words, renderings, or diagrams) that defines us professionally.

The focus on a designer as a stylist—on the visual aspect of design—is not surprising. The visual is our tangible deliverable, and appears to be our greatest (and only) contribution. It is far easier to "critique" and evaluate the physical characteristics of a product rather than debate the products' existence or emotional benefits; we concentrate on the "prettiest" picture instead of the best solution. Designers are traditionally labeled as the "makers" of "pretty things," and as such, we exist at the end of a long process—not where we belong—at the beginning. This placement forces us into a predestined flow dictated by the establishments of marketing, technology, and aesthetics. We are categorically at the whim of conservatism, because, as bizarre, ironic, and paradoxical as it is to the essence of design—designers fear change.

The problem is epidemic; it is not isolated. It is as rampant from academia to Redmond. Our industry and our educational system are both to blame. We both focus considerable time on creating the tangible instead of the intellectual. In addition, the problem is cyclic; academia follows industry and industry is subsequently held hostage by stagnante talent pools.

Professionals spend the majority of their time competing on the level of "cool" instead of the level of "thought." This battle to create the most "bling" is detrimental to designers, to design, and to our clients. Our inability to articulate the importance of process means our clients focus on "money shot" renderings while they overlook the basic testaments of user centric design; moreover, as project managers equate design to "pretty pictures," they gloss over the true usefulness of the discipline: innovation and differentiation.

We must change; we have to become strategists, not just visualists—thinkers, not makers. We need to use our skills of design to solve business problems, not showing how glossy a surface, or how pretty a pixel. We need to move away from being implementers of someone else's ideas to creating opportunities in new markets with our own ideas. Strategy means we as designers need to be broader in our focus. We need to be able to write clearly, to speak eloquently, to substantiate our thoughts, and, of course, to communicate ourselves visually. Furthermore, we need to break down our little walls of comfort and learn to work with people who compliment us: people like writers, researchers, engineers, and executives.

Driven—not driving

Given the current placement of design at the end of the traditional business process, it should not be surprising that design is relegated to stylist. If we are not leading the process with our thoughts, then we will forever follow by "doing the plastics" or "pushing the pixels." Consider how physical products traditionally come to market:

1. A "businessperson" sees an opportunity because he himself has a problem and a deep bank account. A typical suspect is the sole entrepreneur that is so singular in his vision, he forgets that he is in fact, singular. We willingly accept his money, but we have no way to illustrate to him the long-term vision of failure we have seen time and time again.

2. Next, a "marketer" throws out some arbitrary audience description: "design for anyone between eight and eighty." Some form of long-winded but ill-researched documentation accompanies this description; quotes from analysts hardly

compensate for quotes from real people, yet the product requirements document is almost always driven by Forrester or Gartner.

3. An engineer overworks the widget of all widgets, all of the time considering what "he would like."

4. Finally, when the product deadline is looming and the budget is nearly gone, a designer is called in to "make it look good." This stage is easily predicted and includes comments like:

"I know it doesn't make sense, but no, we can't move that, engineering put it there."

"No, it has to be white—the ipod is white; that's what the analysts said."

"User data? No, we don't have any, that's what we pay marketing for."

"I don't care what they want, it's what I want— and I'm paying the bills."

The song remains the same across our industry; you'll find similar stories in the product, graphic, or interactive design consultancy. We are continually beaten down by technology centric and marketing driven initiatives that all end in a visual deliverable. These processes exist because they worked; at one time, the "bar" of user experience was so low that a "not beige" colored plastic was enough to differentiate a product in the marketplace. But as product design drives towards commodity, and the market of goods is more frequently differentiated only by cost, we realize that it is a business decision to turn the process around. Designers need to be facilitators, educators and administrators, but not implementers; they need to be paid for the quality of their ideas, and must be strategically positioned within the organization to do so.

Doers—not thinkers

We live in an industry that has rules, establishments, organizations, and processes that have been developing for the better part of a century. The blame of conservative thinking in design falls equally on all of us, from businesspeople to researchers to educators, but it is the designers that are most at fault for their lack of understanding the business of Design.

Currently, our ability to make money is directly related to production rather than thought. We are compensated based on the quantity of sketches we've produced and the number of hours on the clock, but there is little mention of how well we solved the actual problem at hand. Designers, and design firm owners, get trapped in an unhealthy and uncontrollable cyclical cycle of following the implementation cash cow. We chase jobs that seem lucrative, only to burn through hours quickly: after all, more hours means more clients, and more clients means more money. The work doesn't need to be fulfilling; a beveled edge on the corner of a remote control pays just as well as the beveled edge on the industry blockbuster. Great designers burn out because the work is mediocre; good designers become mediocre designers as they slip into the rut of "bread and butter" design.

Rare is the designer who does not think he could have done a better job. The amount of hubris in the professional industry of design is rampant. Paul Rand, Frank Lloyd Wright, and Philippe Stark are all viewed as "geniuses." Some were, and others still are, tyrannical, often both in personality as well as in their approach to design. These are the figureheads that most equate with design; these "visionaries" are the exception, yet we herald them as the rule.

It is no surprise, then, that designers fear change. We have been taught to be ivory towers unto ourselves—not collaborators or group workers. Fear creeps in from other industries; the young designer is berated with images of Karim Rashid bleating "I want to change the world," yet the consultancy of today allows him to change nothing of substance at all. Who would have thought that an industry that is so focused on change is also so fearful of it? It almost appears as if the progressive and "hip" field of design is the most conservative field of all.

If we pause for a moment and look at similar "knowledge" and "thought-based" industries, we can see the pendulum swings wholly in the other direction. Law is perhaps one of the most profitable (albeit not necessarily moral) businesses for the strategic mind. Computer Scientists, too, are well compensated for their work and their quality of thinking. Computer Scientists, especially, are rewarded by the intellectual property of their thoughts; IPO anyone? Even politicians enjoy some degree of reward based on the quality of their idea.

In short, we have it all backwards. Our inability to assume risk—to change—is, in fact, the biggest risk of all.

No silver bullets

While we need a fundamental change in our philosophy about design and design process, there are many other forces that effect this transition. If "thinking different" were enough, we'd all be using Apple quality products and software. But an obvious barrier to this utopia of "design as strategist" and "designer as leader" is cost: thinking different costs money; sometimes, a lot of money. As is usually the case in business, the more something costs, the less the bean counters want to hear about it.

Thus, communicating—and objectively justifying—our intentions and visions is critical. Communication between all the parties becomes the most critical issue in transitioning design from a skill-based industry to a knowledge-based industry.

The lack of communication in any business context is bait for disaster.

There are two things at consummate odds in our industry: a designer's vision versus the cost of achieving it. The ideal—not idea—that "if you build it, they will come" deserves an asterisk: only if it's affordable, trustworthy, and desirable. We are at odds with our clients. While we want to create ideas, they want to create profits.

Communication in this context does not mean more emails or lengthier phone calls. Communication is the lynchpin of a good design program. It's the difference between good and great; coveted and forgotten; icon and fad. But, how can we improve communication between ourselves, our clients, and our suppliers?

The answer lies in processes we already know. Design is typically described as a visual discipline. However, that is only a partly true. Our discipline has historically welcomed disparate professions into our fold like computer scientists, researchers, cognitive psychologists, and business analysts. Globally, however, we tend to forget that this is a historical precedent, not a trend. As such, we should embrace their best practices and processes to achieve successful communication of our visions. In order to improve, grow, and evolve, we must focus on iterative communication.

1. Don't just listen, start writing. Communication needs to be structured. Help your team by creating communication templates. Templates can range from initial engagement, needs analysis, Persona development, and so on. A formal system of communication involves your clients in the process, ensuring that all parties agree on goals and deliverables, and minimizes redundancy by clearly identifying the boundaries of the scope.

2. Be iterative, cyclical, and consistent, but not occasional. Stop putting so much prominence on the "final presentation." Consider how the software industry relies on short iterative cycles of development rather than a long, drawn out release that climaxes in some pinnacle presentation. For example, a classic industrial design job: a week of late-term development sketching. Over this week, a designer can create about ten quality sketches a day. If we waited for a review, we might have a wall of one hundred sketches. But a review at this stage is too late; even if one of the sketches is acceptable, none of the sketches are refined. Instead, if we are iterative and cyclical, we present—to the client—ten sketches the first day representing our 10 directions. The client can immediately disregard nine of them. This allows us to concentrate on a very specific set of instances, instead of floundering trying to meet our "quota." Moreover, it is a far more strategic approach where "thought" trumps "production." This may seem like an obvious solution; but it's seldom practiced in our industry.

3. Lead by design. Every problem we face is a design problem, and should be approached as such. If a meeting is getting bogged down with a fight over features, take control of the room and consider the problem from a "design point of view": write the ideas down and begin to find connections between ideas. If a marketing or businessperson is struggling to communicate an idea, sketch it. We all too often forget about our strongest assets when we're in meetings with non-designers. Yet, it is these times when it is most important to remember the power of design thinking.

Thinking is the new black

There is a reason why computer scientists, doctors, architects, and lawyers are wealthy: they use their brains as their bartering tools. They are knowledge workers and strategists, and while they all "create," they are not *only implementers*. Daily, we sell ourselves short by allowing ourselves to be described as "makers." An architect certainly does not describe himself as a draftsperson; we must lead with our minds—not with our pencils.

Design strategy is comprehensive. It is far deeper than the superficiality of brand strategy. "Make it all white, like the ipod" is about as far from design strategy as one can get. Strategy is the ability for design to unite all the members of the product development process: Business, Marketing, Engineering, Research, and Clients. We are the glue that ties all these parts together, and the grease that makes them move freely and quickly. We, as a discipline, need to be active in demanding a more responsible role in the design process.

Business (and design) has long been overseen by "project managers": people who lust over timetables, budgets, and specs. Innovation does not exist where time and budgets are commodities. Design needs to sit where it is most useful, in the beginning, as a strategic tool; a place where vision and the future are paramount. This place is as close to the CEO as possible. Jay Mays at Ford, Jonathan Ives at Apple, and Michael Graves with Target have all clearly illustrated the power of design as a strategic business motivator.

Enter the Interaction Designer

While the end goal may be "designer as board member," the interim solution is to utilize the Interaction Designer as program manager.

A Designer as manager is an invaluable asset. The strongest quality a designer can possess is the ability to empathize with people and understand their needs. The first rule of good design is to understand your audience; this applies when developing a product, but it also applies when facilitating in the boardroom.

Designers have the uncanny ability to think above a situation and yet continually judge the ramifications of a group decision. This is extremely different from traditional project managers, people who may have gained their position because of their abilities to balance a budget or build a spreadsheet. A good designer looks at everyone's position at once; he is able to remain un-mired in engineering's rat-holes or marketing's hyperactive vernacular jargon speak.

A Designer as strategist can take seemingly disparate haystacks of information and rearrange them to make sense—even to someone who is a layman. Consider the principles of information architecture applied not to a website but to an entire corporation. Along with empathizing with people's problems, good designers can organize schedules and deliverables, group tasks, and arrange ideas far more creatively than any other discipline. Designers are built to recognize disparate patterns across verticals. This is invaluable when developing products that span different mediums, such as a digital music player that interacts with a software application.

A Designer is a generalist. Once well educated and experienced, they understand all areas of the product development process and their effect on the overall product. In fact, as design education continues to evolve, the lines are blurred between communication, industrial, interactive, and interior design. While there will certainly always be specialists who concentrate in one area, a new breed of designers—those who focus on the overall experience of a product—are becoming more relevant. Within these people is the knowledge of multiple design disciplines; these people consider the interaction—or experience—one has with a product (moreover a Brand), and are able to see the forest and the trees.

These new designers understand business. They know what it takes to make money; they understand their audience and design for their needs. They understand the ramifications of technology, engineering constraints, and materials science. Finally, they know that their audience needs to be able to purchase their products; they understand the power of the internet, marketing, and the new retail experience. This designer is at the same time technical and creative, pragmatic and visionary.

A designer has a tool belt of skills that is as much art as it is science. Design can seem magical: designers have the ability to make the intangible real. The designer's innate ability to empathize with people, organize tasks, synthesize information, and think laterally makes him the most valuable asset in an organization.

Implementing strategy

I have pursued this vision of Interaction Designer in upper management relentlessly over the past 5 years. From my experience, I have discovered three activities which must be employed to achieve this vision successfully. They work serially to build upon each other, and they are not easy.

1. Philosophize. Change the way people think. The biggest barrier to successfully implementing a new process based on design is the philosophical change the organization has to go through. This is unequivocally the most difficult task of the three.

Designers are conservative, and worse, territorial. This is true in other disciplines as well, and no one wants to be told they now need to be subservient to a new set of practices. The last thing a Principal of a company wants to hear is how broken his business is. However, if you can convince him that the opportunity far outweighs the fear, then you can begin to gain ground; Philosophizing must begin at the top.

One must convince the "powers that be" that this is the way of the future. In order to do this, the process must be clear, concise, and substantiated: the process must be directly related to the bottom line. Prior success speaks volumes; in order to illustrate prior success, those successes must be documented.

While philosophizing, one can expect to hear defensive prattle like:

"We've always done business like this, no need to change."

"You're a "make it pretty" guy, you don't know about business."

"I'm smart; I don't need to know what users think. I'm smarter than them."

"You can't sell that here, we're a product company— we don't need research."

"I don't need strategy. I use my business intuition— it's better than any of your research."

To quiet the naysayers, one must be extremely clear how Interaction Design will be integrated, will positively effect business, and will be utilized. The best way to illustrate these is to allow your audience to find them on their own: empower your executives to think. Help them see design as an answer to their struggles.

2. Indoctrinate. Once people understand that change is coming, it's time to make your team, company, and boss believe in the "force" in order to make it happen. Here is where designers do what they do best: visually communicate the Philosophy. Put simply: make a diagram and create a vision.

Almost all organizations have some degree of problems related to business, culture, workflow, and process. Our goal as designers is to solve these through simplicity. Utilize design to communicate these problems and to show how the natural process of design implicitly solves these problems. A good business process diagram will show who the stakeholders are, where they affect the process, and how each stakeholder interacts with each other. At this stage, your goal is to address the specific concerns of people throughout your organization. You need to indoctrinate them not only with the philosophy of design, but also with its vernacular, process, and ideals. In short, begin to address specific concerns from above:

"We've always done business like this, no need to change."

Show that the addition of integrated design services will help to add bottom line results by expanding the business at the front end, and then throughout the process. Further, show that core business has been eroded steadily because of their "lack of change," cheap outsourcing, and shift of the industry away from implementation.

"You're a "make it pretty" guy, you don't know about business."

Show that designers understand "people," and people buy products. Thus, we know quite a lot about what appeals, what constitutes a good market opportunity, and how to drive innovation early in a process; this increases the likelihood of getting to market early, generating intellectual property, and increasing market share.

"I'm smart, I don't need to know what users think. I'm smarter than them."

Arrogance is a recipe for disaster. Anytime the "I'm an expert" argument is raised, inquire how over-budget the program was, how successful the product was, and how many times did work need to be done over. Moreover, how happy was the client? Strategy is the insurance policy for the designer. If we are clear in our vision, we will be clear in our designs.

"You can't sell that here, we're a product company— we don't need research or strategy."

Design can be infused in any organization, from a real estate agency to a potato farm; nearly all business case studies accurately describe design, yet use words that are familiar to the MBA. Reframe a traditional business case in light of strategic design and planning.

"I don't need strategy. I use my intuition— it's better than any of your research."

If your organization traditionally does a one-eighty every development cycle because they wait till they have a product nearly complete before they talk to users, show them how design will put the user first; illustrate how research and strategy won't cramp their style, but in fact will bolster productivity by providing a framework for innovation.

Why use a diagram to convey all of this critical information?

The answer is simple; it holds us accountable. It ties us to a formal communication of our intentions; it disseminates easily, and it allows us to create a repetitious call to action. Our goal is to educate and indoctrinate an organization about design philosophy by showcasing how designers solve problems: creatively, visually, and tangibly. By being visual, it forces problems into the open. Principals, naysayers, and mediocre staff can't hide behind three by five foot printouts. A good visual solution to this problem stirs communication, creates momentum, and drives change. It positions the designer as a thinker, something the organization may have had no previous exposure to.

3. Entrench. The difficult job becomes harder; you must establish your relationship to the core competencies of the business. Identify the area you can "own," and expand from there. In a product design company, attach yourself to something that is as close to the audience as possible: the controls, buttons, materials, icons, and ultimately, the audience. You may find yourself doing more communication design than Interaction Design at the start, but it is a means to an end.

This process may take months—or even years. It is tedious, time consuming, and personally exhausting. But when all is said and done, you have successfully "laddered up" from simply impacting individual programs to creating strategic recommendations for future markets.

It's Design, not design

Being a designer should be one of the most rewarding careers a thought leader can pursue. For some of us, it certainly comes close. It's fulfilling, irresistible, and enthralling when it goes well. Yet we still face an uphill battle, and many of us will tire of the constant evangelism necessary to gain the respect we deserve. Each of us is responsible for making the whole of the industry—nay, the world—understand the importance of design. It is not enough to make things prettier; we need to make them more "usable, useful, and desirable." We need to educate our co-workers, our friends across the globe, ourselves, and we must be relentless in the communication of this education. Else, we run the risk of selling ourselves short, undermining our worth, and remaining just "makers" and not "thinkers."

Henry Ford said it best: "There is no man living who isn't capable of doing more than he thinks he can do." Henry must have been talking about a Designer.

Copyright for this article is held by Justin Petro; reprinted here with permission.

SECTION THREE

3

THE RHETORICAL NATURE OF INTERACTION DESIGN

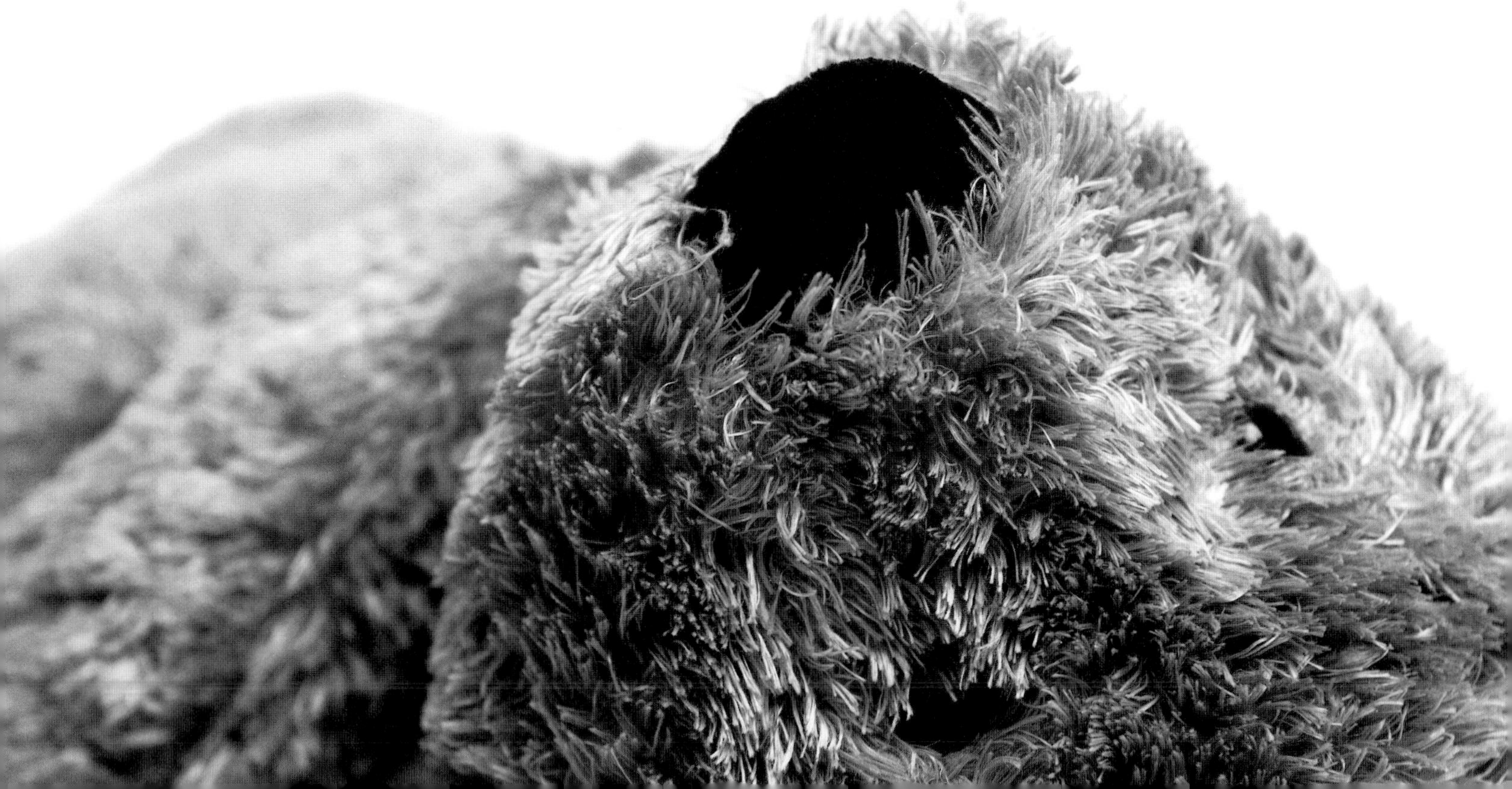

Interaction Design is married to language, as design is synonymous with communication. To create a compelling behavior means to have a cohesive dialogue with a person, and in order to speak with a person, a designer must first know, respect, and understand a bit about that person. Think of the alienation that occurs in a foreign land where one does not speak the native language. The sense of anxiety, yet the embrace of possibility is the same space that a person encounters when first discovering a "designed interaction."

A designer does not simply create an object. The importance of understanding the long-term dialogue that occurs with a product focuses around the cultural methods of use and misuse that a person engages in with this object. Indeed, long-term dialogue may be exponentially more important than short-term usability. Consider a teddy bear. The bear becomes worn, loved, the nose bitten off, the seams begin to sag. This bear has spoken, as has the user, and the course of the dialogue has created a relationship between inanimate (albeit highly personified) object and human. The language the bear speaks engages words as emotion. We understand the bear as an object, yet we love it as if it were human.

The communication of language can be considered on a level of content, and can also be thought of on a level of clarity. How well is the message, whatever it may be, disseminated? Has the "styling" been corrupted through poor materials or lost in translation as the product traveled to China to be manufactured? Does the message communicated through software make sense when viewed in light of the hardware?

While the previous chapters have discussed a framework for considering Interaction Design as the design of behavior, this section analyzes the more rhetorical views of Interaction Design. The role of language is examined as it relates to the design of objects, services, and systems. Traditional views of design as dialogue are extended to investigate the role of a poetic interaction—and how designers can begin to view their creations in terms of dialogue, words, and argument.

CHAPTER SIX:
INTERACTION DESIGN AND COMMUNICATION

If "a picture is worth a thousand words," consider the worth, in words, of a product. Are the products in your house talking? What are they saying?

The designer as persuader

Design can be thought of as a form of communication. This does not imply that combining shapes into forms is like combining letters into words. Instead, a designer associates and embeds existing words into his design, which then becomes a proxy for the designer himself. This view of design language is the view of designer as persuader. This is discussed at length by Richard Buchanan in his text "Declaration by Design: Rhetoric, Argument, and Demonstration in Design Practice."[56] Buchanan explains that all forms of design encompass some aspect of rhetoric, or argument. These are defined either by the individual designer's world view or design philosophy, or by the overarching social world of design (which could be thought of as corporate policy or branding). As technology becomes more influential in pushing product innovation, successful design rhetoric—or persuasive language—becomes immensely important.

A product does not only speak but in fact attempts to convince—a designer makes an argument that comes alive each time a person considers his creation. Buchanan argues that designers can not help but persuade, and technology is often used as smoke and mirrors to insert an empty dialogue. But instead of relying on the "coolness" of technology, form, material, and function can be successfully combined to create a cohesive argument. A pursuit of argument can be viewed as an attempt to shape one's attitude. Design is to communicate, and this communication is not a monologue. It is a dialogue of persuasion, and argument, and learning.

Rhetorical argument implies a sense of purpose: "Indeed, design is an art of communication on two levels: It attempts to persuade audiences not only that a given design is useful, but also that the designer's premises or attitudes and values regarding practical life or the proper role of technology are important, as well."[57] A designer may develop the next generation of cell phones, dealing with the physical form of the telephone, the material and manufacturing choices, as well as the software interface that a user encounters to perform calls. This designer's communication can be viewed on several levels; on a highly superficial level, it is possible to discuss the implications of using brushed aluminum and long, slender lines to illustrate a sense of futurism and references to technology in architecture. A deeper analysis might consider the "usability" of the phone—has the designer created a well-structured dialogue, so the user and object can communicate efficiently and effectively? Finally, it is possible to consider the argument the designer has made by choosing to design cellular communication at all. They may be—implicitly, obviously—making a statement concerning the benefits technology has awarded society with rapid communication across geographical boundaries. Or, the commentary may be considered more trivial: The designer may be simply stating that they "Prefer to Make Cool Things."

56   Buchanan, Richard, "Declaration by Design: Rhetoric, Argument, and Demonstration in Design Practice" in *Design Discourse: History, Theory, Criticism*. Ed Victor Margolin. The University of Chicago Press, 1989. p111.

57   Ibid.

As another example of design rhetoric and argument, reflect on the form of a music-playing device. Specifically, picture a portable audio tape player. What does it look like?

Most will envision a similar—and archetypical—image of a square device with a clear panel in it. It is easy to picture the small spools that twist the tape around, and this imagery allows an easy conceptualization of how the object functions. The cognitive accessibility of the device's functionality makes it predictable. In addition to simply picturing the item, most people—however technical—can form some sort of mental model of how the device works. This mental model may be technically inaccurate, but it allows for a quick analysis of the essential method of operation. The rhetorical stance taken by the designer (be it a designer at Sony or a designer at Aiwa) is probably going to be fairly similar.

This same sort of analysis can be performed with a portable compact disc player. Most people have a fairly clear understanding of the formal characteristics of a CD player that have been driven by the functional characteristics of a CD. The device is flat, and roughly the size of the compact disc. Arguing that "form follows function" leaves little room for the individual aesthetics of brand (the color of the plastic, or the placement of the buttons), but the general archetypical form resonates easily with the audience. A CD player is a CD player.

Now consider an MP3 player. What does it look like? A more difficult question may be: What *should* it look like? In this case, the pliability of digital technology affords huge leniency with regard to form, material, size, color, and weight. The designer is not constrained to follow a mechanically driven function, and must instead make decisions based on external characteristics. An MP3 player can look like anything at all: It can be a square white box with radiused corners and a round click wheel in the middle, or it can be shaped like a carrot. The importance of persuasion—of convincing an audience that the MP3 player is "correctly designed"—increases dramatically when functionality is nearly invisible. All too often, this rhetoric is left up to the advertisers—who may resort to brute force tactics of persuasion in loud television ads or huge billboards. But argument, either through form or advertising, need not be loud. Would the iPod succeed without the subtle and refined Dancing Silhouettes reminding us that Apple has discovered the "proper" form for an MP3 player? The argument of this advertising campaign, combined with the care and attention to detail of the physical iPod, has created a rather ubiquitous "sign" of what an MP3 player should look like.

Designed artifacts identify an underlying culture

Designers Shelley Evenson and John Rheinfrank[58] established, through years of designing product and systems at consultancies like Scient, the Doblin Group, and Fitch, a theory of visual and functional product language. Like Buchanan, Evenson and Rheinfrank considered language as the strong connector between artifacts and people, and discussed how design languages become a connector for how people experience products, services, and systems in the world around them. People do not simply *use* product form language—they *live* with it. Product form language

58 The late John Rheinfrank can also be credited with the definition of Interaction Design as accepted in this text. He was a principle at Doblin Group, an Executive Vice President at Fitch, and a professor at Carnegie Mellon University, Illinois Institute of Technology, and the Kellogg School of Management. He also began the publication *Interactions*, offered by the ACM, which is still the only notable publication discussing topics of Interaction Design without resorting to the more mundane and pragmatic view of Interface Design, GUI Design or Web Design.

is the basis for how people generate and interpret their surroundings. This has great implications for the design of mass-produced items. These items do more than simply provide a function or some form of functional utility. When viewed under the guise of language, these products become the fabric of society, and allow people to express themselves, to communicate with others, and to shape their environment in unique ways.

Evenson and Rheinfrank were referring to the physical form, material, and visual style of an artifact. Products that incorporate an extended level of digitization (and, therefore, complexity) often seem confusing based on their visual aesthetic. It is difficult for people to rationally consider and analyze a personal video recorder because the form language surrounding the recorder is often arbitrary—perhaps inspired by older, analog recorders, or inspired by the whim of the designer. One way to think about the way

a designer may impact culture, then, is to analyze the language and style in which a digital object is presented. The Interaction Designer shapes culture directly through the creation of new visual form language. This semantic view of design—that objects are embedded with more than just functional significance—rejects the platitude of Form Follows Function and instead recognizes the need for emotional and social connections in the human-made world.

This view is formally grounded in the study of semiotics. Semiotics is, literally, the study of signs. A sign need not be a printed object, but instead can include the theoretical understanding of the process of *signification*. By signifying something (or signing as a verb), humans can communicate meaning, and a sign itself is thought to carry some form of meaning. The sign (either physical or conceptual) uses various codes to help communicate the meaning and values embedded within it. A sign can be a visual element—like a street sign—but can also be the way one uses his body language, or the sound pattern of words used to communicate to another. [59]

Ferdinand de Saussure is generally considered the founder of the semiotic movement. He considered language as a scientific and independent notion that could be separated from elements of culture or comprehension. Saussure believed that words are embedded with semantic meaning and therefore "stand for" other things—the word "chair" (in any human, spoken language) is deeply associated with the idea of sitting and the idea of the object that we sit on. The rules that make up the system become universally more important than the application of the rules—that is, the notion of "chairness" exists whether or not we are using, considering, or speaking about a "chair." One can consider and theorize on the nature of signs independent of particular usages or examples. [60]

If *designed artifacts* (such as objects like chairs or even complicated computer interfaces) follow Saussure's view of semiotics—and are thought of as signs rather than as simple physical and static elements of function—one can start to understand that the process of signification is deeply related to Interaction Design and the process of behavioral understanding in experiences. This might include the name of the object (often arbitrary—what does a "DVD player" really mean?), the body movements necessary to manipulate the object (the sunken, press-able nature of buttons, or the round and "turnable" style of a dial), or the proper way to consider an object ("I am a serious piece of consumer electronics. Do not play with me.") A sign, by definition, should be fairly universal and easy to understand. One should not require training to comprehend the message being communicated (in fact, semiotics frequently implies that users can't *help* but be affected by the process of signification—it happens automatically).

---

59 "A linguistic sign is not a link between a thing and a name, but between a concept and a sound pattern. The sound pattern is not actually a sound, for a sound is something physical. A sound pattern is the hearer's psychological impression of a sound, as given to him by the evidence of his senses. This sound pattern may be called a 'material' element only in that it is the representation of our sensory impressions. The sound pattern may thus be distinguished from the other element associated with it in a linguistic sign. This other element is generally of a more abstract kind: the concept." Saussure, Ferdinand de, *Course in General Linguistics* (trans. Roy Harris). London: Duckworth).

60 As if this isn't complicated enough, many notable contributors to the field of linguistics have subsequently critiqued this rigid notion that the structure of language can be separated from its use; contextualizing language seems to change meaning, as was pointed out by Valentin Voloshinov (Voloshinov, Valentin, *Marxism and the Philosophy of Language* (trans. Ladislav Matejka & I R Titunik). Seminar Press, 1973)—Voloshinov felt that the "sign is part of organized social interchange and cannot exist, as such, outside it." Voloshinov theorized that the meaning of a sign is not as related to other signs, but instead to the way it is used—to the actual context of use.

Design language can provide the cultural substance

While there certainly is a market for "cool things," some designers find the emphasis on styling and visual aesthetics as superficial—a great deal of the design community feels that a designer provides a deeply intellectual contribution in the creation of goods, and the sensory elements are only the most immediate "hook" for people to respond to a creation. In fact, there is much more substance to designed artifacts, and it is this substance that allows them to resonate in a meaningful fashion. This substance is what Saussure viewed as the linguistic sign, what Evenson and Rheinfrank viewed as a design language, and what Buchanan considered as the harmonious combination of rational, human, and stylistic.

One way of examining and considering this level of substance is through a linguistic lens of *poetry*. An interaction occurs in the conceptual space between a person and an object. It is at once physical, cognitive, and social. A *poetic* interaction is one that resonates immediately but yet continues to inform later—it is one that causes reflection, and one that relies heavily on a state of *emotional awareness*. Additionally, a poetic interaction is one that is nearly always subtle, yet mindful.

Consider the poetic and highly refined act of chopping a clove of garlic with a Wüsthof cook's knife—and compare it to the obvious, jarring experience of riding a roller coaster through the most perilous curves. The roller coaster drops and turns, and relies on the adrenalin rush associated with near death. It creates an experience so riddled with awe that many will stop "thinking" at all. Each turn and drop is bigger than the last, and as riders feel the wind in their hair and the blood in their ears, the exhilaration is one that is sensory and perceptual first and cognitive second, if ever.

By comparison, preparing a meal can be a rather banal experience. Imagine using the heavy forged steel Wüsthof, the cold metal against your hand, the staccato and constant motion of the blade against the cutting board, and the pungent odor of garlic pressing against your eyes and nose. This mundane experience described is a story, which creates, much like a compelling novel, a world for the participant to engage in. Unlike a novel, however, the participant is not an idle observer. The active engagement of the senses encourages a highly heightened sense of awareness[61]—the "user" is not simply a "viewer."

The roller-coaster forces a set of behavior through brute force, and reminds the rider over and over that he is, in fact, thrilled. The knife, by comparison, speaks quietly but firmly. The interaction is at once less obvious and more compelling. The entertainment provided by the roller-coaster is passive in the most obvious sense—a rider sits, and his senses are assaulted. The "entertainment" provided by the knife is highly active, demanding a sense of acute engagement.

....

61   Don Norman discusses this in his text *Emotional Design*, and makes a brief and fleeting reference to Poetry: "Here is the power of storytelling, of the script, the actors, transporting viewers into the world of make-believe. This is 'the willful suspension of disbelief' that the English poet Samuel Taylor Coleridge discussed as being essential for poetry. Here is where you get captured, caught up in the story, identifying with the situation and the characters" (Norman, 125, reprinted with permission). This common link seems to connect the fields of poetry, cinema, and design. Understanding the poetics of Interaction Design, then, can hardly be an isolated undertaking. It must be interdisciplinary, and the Interaction Designer must be worldy aware.

A poetic interaction can generally be characterized as having, or encouraging, three main elements: honesty, mindfulness, and a vivid and refined attention to sensory detail. These elements combine to encourage creativity in the end participant (note the shift away from the word *user*, as the audience no longer simply *uses* but instead must *actively engage*).

The honesty of poetic interactions

Honesty is a difficult word to discuss as applied to product development, as it brings to mind issues of ethics, morality, and the basic axioms of humanity. While the principles of life, liberty, and the pursuit of happiness resonate with Americans, these are ideologically Western views—thoughts of simplicity, respect, and nature may make more sense to the Japanese. Thus, while underlying and basic principles of integrity (do not steal, do not kill) may transcend cultures, the details of honesty seem to be culturally independent. Products that attempt to convey a sense of honesty may, in fact, not make any sense when presented in other cultures (and sub-cultures) and communities. Given that culture changes over time, honest product design, too, may begin to alter depending on the momentum of society.

All cannot be relative, however, if the attempt is to define a framework for poetic Interaction Design. If honesty implies integrity, Interaction Designers can uphold the integrity of several aspects of the design through the development of the product, and these particular aspects of honesty seem to transcend cultural boundaries: integrity to the business vision, integrity to the consumer, and integrity to materials.

Frequently, business decisions are made with a great deal of thought and consideration, yet the dissemination of these goals is thwarted by tiers of middle management that twist and convolute both the decision and the rationale for that decision. To uphold integrity to the business vision requires that Interaction Designers participate in the development of this business vision in some manner. How can one uphold the integrity of something if one isn't aware of what that something is? Internal corporate branding, often represented as a set of strategic imperatives or as a set of goal-outcome statements, is used to disseminate business objectives internally. These statements are often an obvious attempt to force a value system on a set of participants who had little to do with the creation of these values. Jim Clemmer,[62] author of *Firing on All Cylinders*, claims that these imperatives are "those vital 12 to 18 month goals, priorities, and improvement targets that—when reached—hurl our team or organization towards its vision, value and purpose." Yet most involved in the develop-ment of products cringe when they hear a goal or priority broken down into a tongue-in-cheek euphemism like "Trim the Fat" (Albertsons) or into single, staccato like bullets of "Imagine. Build. Solve. Lead." (General Electric). These miniature rallying cries rely on rote memorization and belittle the audience—they implicitly state that members of a company can't understand the complexity of business decisions and strategy.

62   Clemmer is egregiously self-labeled as a "bestselling author and internationally acclaimed keynote speaker, workshop/retreat leader, and management team developer on leadership, change, customer focus, culture, teams, and personal growth" <http://www.clemmer.net/excerpts/use_strategic.shtml>

Victor Margolin reflects that "Designer/entrepreneurs should be able to create business plans, identify niches for new products within the global marketplace, and seek appropriate venture capital."[63] If designers and artists truly understand why they are working on a particular project or direction, they can best embrace the strategic decision and "hurl" themselves forward at it. This understanding of business value and strategy requires equal representation at the heart of business: **A designer needs to be present in the boardroom, where these decisions are made.**

Integrity to the consumer, or participant, requires the passionate advocacy for humanity. This advocacy transcends "making things user friendly" or "foolproof," and instead requires respect for the end consumers and "users" of the product.[64] This respect comes from understanding and empathy, and results in a level of commitment that often relies on the emotive instead of the rational. While design and manufacturing are engaged in for-profit activities, these activities should be ethical and informed. The entire notion of "planned obsolescence" rejects this notion of integrity for humanity, in that it attempts to pull the wool over the naïve consumers' eyes. Industrial Designer Brooks Stevens has been recognized as coining the term *planned obsolescence*. Consider the subtle audacity of his definition for this quality of design: "Instilling in the buyer the desire to own something a little newer, a little better, a little sooner than is necessary."[65] With design comes a great deal of power. Rather than attempting to trick otherwise neutral participants in the dialogue of a product, why not exert this power toward the creation of betterment for the individual, his family, and his society?

Integrity to materials requires a sense of respect for both the natural world and the human-made world, and the philosophical understanding of how various materials *want* to work. Consider a PT Cruiser with wood paneling (wood laminate, a thin sheet of wood or a wood-like material) on the side. The car is made of metal and plastic, and is artificial in nearly every way (even in its allusions to early Sixties wagons). According to Chrysler, it is the "small car alternative that lives large." Why, then, would a designer specify a choice of "a simple, flowing wood-grained graphic" on the doors, the graphic being "a linear Medium Oak woodgrain framed with Light Ash surround moldings"? The car isn't wooden, and in this case, the *wood* isn't even wooden! Trevor Creed, Senior Vice President of Design at the Chrysler Group, attempts to explain that "For the Chrysler PT Cruiser 'Woodie' Edition, we wanted a design execution that recreated the carefree fun of the popular 1960s California surf wagons."[66] But the popular California surf wagons, specifically the Mercury Station Wagon, *were* made of solid wood. The 1946 Mercury Woodie was made of a solid wood frame (most probably birch or mahogany), as were many vehicles in

---

63 Margolin, Victor. "The Designer as Producer" in *Citizen Designer: Perspectives on Design Responsibility*. Ed Steven Heller. Watson-Guptill Publications, 2003.

64 It is interesting to compare the idea of Advocacy to that of Usability Engineering. Advocacy implies a human voice and a strong, active commitment towards betterment. Usability Engineering, on the other hand, frequently takes either a technical perspective or a business perspective, resorting to percentages of usability improvements or a cost justification for usability activities. Advocacy cannot be polluted by compromise, which is inherent in the embracement of technical or business rationale in justifying one's existence in the product development cycle.

65 Adamson, Glenn. *Industrial Strength Design. How Brooks Stevens Shaped Your World*. MIT Press, 2003.

66 Creed, Trevor. September 20, 2001. Press release.

the late thirties and early forties. If a car is going to be made of wood, it should deserve to be made of wood. What type of design deserves to be made of a "wood-grained graphic"?

One can't help but think of the idealistic Ayn Rand's Howard Roark, as he denounces the Parthenon as poorly architected: "The famous flutings on the famous columns—what are they made for? To hide the joints in wood—when columns were made of wood, only these aren't, they're marble… Your Greeks took marble and they made copies of their wooden structures out of it, because others had done it that way. Then your masters of the Renaissance came along and made copies in plaster of copies in marble of copies in wood. Now here we are, making copies in steel and concrete of copies in plaster of copies in marble of copies in wood…"[67]

Sustainable Design advocates William McDonough and Michael Braungart illustrate a similar respect for materials and the associated principle of honesty in design in the physical manifestation of their text *Cradle to Cradle*. The pages of the text are made of plastic, rather than paper. The ink from the pages can easily be washed and captured for re-use. The plastic itself can be reused without downcycling. As McDonough wondered aloud during the Industrial Designers Society of America annual conference in Washington, DC, in 2005, "Why make something as simple as a sheet of paper out of something as elegant as a tree? Design something that makes oxygen, fixes nitrogen, build soil, provides habitat for hundreds of people, and self replicates… and cut it down to write on it?"[68]

Investigating mindfulness

In addition to the elements of honesty, a poetic interaction should encourage a state of mindfulness. Mindfulness (note the subtle distinction between mindfulness and mindlessness) has often been cited as the primary state of mind necessary to accomplish meditation. Buddhists reference a state of mindfulness of breathing. One can think of mindfulness as an acute awareness of the present moment.[69] Rather than actively considering other people, or chores that need to be done, or opinions that need to be formed, one simply exists, and understands this moment of that existence. This appreciation for the present moment has been cited as a successful method by marathon runners and artists alike, and discussed by authors such as Ralph Waldo Emerson and Walt Whitman.

A successful poetic Interaction Design will encourage a state of mindfulness. This is, of course, easier said than done. To achieve this state of mental appreciation, one must be willing (and actively choose) to ignore many of the problems and elements present in the hustle of daily life. How can a product encourage a user to let go of his surroundings and attend only to the moment?

When reading a poem, it is interesting to consider where the imagery comes from. The words on the page are rather plain, and save for the authors' potential use of kitschy typography, the print itself is rather nondescript. Words themselves frequently fail to trigger vivid and robust

---

67 Rand, Ayn. *The Fountainhead*. Signet, 50th Annv edition, 1996. p24.

68 McDonough's quote is taken from the IDSA keynote address in Washington, DC, although he has made this point in many other talks as well.

69 Author Jon Kabat-Zinn offers a more poetic description of mindfulness in his book *Wherever You Go, There You Are*: "Mindfulness means paying attention in a particular way: on purpose, in the present moment, and nonjudgmental. This kind of attention nurtures greater awareness, clarity, and acceptance of present-moment reality. It wakes us up to the fact that our lives unfold only in moments." Copyright © 1994 Jon Kabat-Zinn; reprinted by permission of Hyperion. All rights reserved.

thoughts, as the brain seems to desire to think in two dimensions. That is, even when trying passionately to picture a "tree in the rain," few readers will get beyond the prototypical form of a tree—the form that, perhaps, a child will scrawl when asked to draw a tree. This lack of ability to visualize an object in full detail in the mind may be what holds many back from claiming artistic capabilities. "I can't draw" usually means "I can't draw accurately," and it may be more appropriate to claim "I can't think" (or at least "I can't think accurately").

But compare the imagery conjured by a "tree in the rain", to this short excerpt from "The Wasteland":

> *April is the cruellest month, breeding*
> *Lilacs out of the dead land, mixing*
> *Memory and desire, stirring*
> *Dull roots with spring rain*[70]

T. S. Eliot has managed to use the same basic constructs of words, and simple words at that, to stir deep emotional responses in the reader. A "tree in the rain" is finite, obvious, and non-challenging. The lack of complexity and specificity may, in fact, be why it is difficult to picture the tree with any depth or detail. But the fact that the lilac has dead roots, and it isn't just a rain—it's a *spring* rain, creates a matter-of-fact situation that readers can begin to feel, before they even try to *see* it. It is difficult to picture April, much less to picture the month as cruel, yet Eliot's four lines have managed to invigorate a deeply honed sense of feeling that allows readers to picture not just a tree, nor a rain, but an entire scene.

In much the same way as readers have difficulty picturing a "tree in the rain" with any level of character, they may have a similarly troubling time imagining opening a car door, or turning on the television, or typing an email. Simply recalling the nature of interactions one has had throughout the day is a particularly difficult task, in a peculiarly striking way. As an example, try to imagine how many doors you must have opened, how many buttons you have pressed in one day. Surely there were a lot, but recreating these actions or recalling particulars is incredibly difficult. It may be difficult to reproduce these ideas because they happened, for lack of a better word, automatically. It is not necessary to consciously attend to the car door when encountering it. Your focus was most likely on the destination of the drive, or the other passengers in the car. Most will recall actual behavior only when it fails. It is easy to recall when the door broke, or when a key was lost, or when a door was difficult to open.

Author, psychologist, and philosopher John Dewey explains that "Experience does not go on simply inside a person. It does go on there, for it influences the formation of attitudes of desire and purpose. But this is not the whole of the story. Every genuine experience has an active side which changes in some degree the objective conditions under which experiences are had."[71] This implies that, while an Interaction Designer may focus on the creation of an artifact or system, much of the "meat" of the experience of use is left up to the person *using* the artifact or system. This lack of control in design can be frightening, especially for the designer who is used to thinking of design as an expressive, personal, and highly

70   T. S. Eliot, "The Wasteland".

71   Dewey, John. *Experience and Education*. Free Press, Reprint Edition. 1997. p39.

finite activity. In fact, thinking of design as an activity of creation (a verb) with a beginning and an end ignores the entire beauty of the engagement with the *person* for which a design (a noun) was created in the first place.

Frequently, resonant interactions are creative interactions with a heightened awareness of task. Author and psychologist Mihaly Csikszentmihalyi has been analyzing the essence of creativity, and has identified the state of being known as "flow" to be one that encourages a vivid awareness of the moment but an almost lack of awareness of the surrounding environment and task. As Csikszentmihalyi describes, during flow, the sense of self and self-consciousness disappears. While experiencing flow, people become too involved in their activities to worry about protecting their self-image or their ego.[72]

Perhaps, then, it is useful to attempt to recall not a particular interaction but the beauty of the associative scene. In the same way that a poem requires a sense of whole in order to understand the parts, so too does a successful interaction require both a holistic attention to the context and a dramatically detailed understanding of nuance.

Providing a vivid and refined attention to sensory detail

In addition to honesty and mindfulness, a vivid and refined attention to sensory detail can be thought of as the last necessary element to encourage a poetic and resonant Interaction Design. This attention to sensory detail—made up of all elements of design, including material, form, color, texture, placement—is frequently lost during the translation from

concept to reality in the actual development of manufactured goods. Two main explanations can be cited for the loss of this important quality: an understanding of importance, and cost.

Often, the folks working in product development don't understand, respect, or care about attention to sensory details. Many engineers and business executives have a difficult time embracing the subjective benefits of one material over the other. This is not to say that engineers and executives don't care about *all* details; indeed, to achieve a level of Six Sigma quality, engineers *must* be detail driven.[73] But these details are in logic and in process, rather than in the visual or the aesthetic. Many engineers simply have not been trained to perceive these details. Those who have designed computer interfaces can attest to the blinders software developers have towards visual style. To many developers, the user interface is an inconvenience, and one that commonly implies drastic compromises and delays in development. It is not accidental that one can achieve a B.S. in Computer Science at Carnegie Mellon University and never take a required user interface development course. The design of visual control interfaces are relegated to an elective.

Additionally, issues of cost frequently disrupt attention to sensory detail. In the development of a physical product, designers may specify very particular trim pieces or premium surface treatments. These details will help differentiate a product in the marketplace and will serve to create a cohesive experience of use, but will also add cost to the development of the product. In a business culture, the value of these particular ephemeral enhancements may simply not be comprehensible to the managers mak-

---

72 Csikszentmihalyi, Mihaly. *Creativity : Flow and the Psychology of Discovery and Invention.* Harper Perennial, 1997. p112.

73 Six Sigma is a quality management program that originated with Motorola; the program attempts to measure and reduce defects in the mass production of products.

ing financial decisions. These details are at the heart of popular industrial design successes like the Apple iPod, the Motorola RAZR, and the Audi TT. Imagine the iPod in a cheaper grade of plastic, or the TT without the hallmark—and more expensive—art deco gauges and custom leather interior. Companies like Apple and Audi continually understand and respect attention to detail in visual aesthetics, and frequently pass on the cost of this refinement to the consumer, who will happily pay the premium price to enjoy the premium experience.

To resonate poetic, the interaction one has with a product should be engaging, appropriately complicated to the given task in order to encourage a mindful state, and highly sensory. But it is important to note that the moment need not be *long*. While pouring a cup of coffee out of a French press, one may experience a mindful interaction, if only for several seconds. The combination of acuity necessary to perform the task (the challenge, if you like, of successfully moving the hot coffee from one apparatus to another), and the appropriate materials (stainless steel, glass) and the various sensory elements (the smell of the rich coffee, the heat against the pouring hand, the billows of steam from the bottom of the coffee mug) creates a poetic interaction.

A poetic interaction may not be a usable interaction

It is interesting to note that none of the traits outlined above—honesty, mindfulness, or sensory refinement—has much to do with usability, or with common usability metrics. Usability is usually associated with decreasing time necessary to *complete* a task (and increasing efficiency), decreasing the time necessary to *learn* a new interface, or *reducing* number of errors. Usability engineering commonly recommends a reduction of cognitive demands, and seems to encourage the creation of "mindless" interfaces that simply don't require a great deal of thought to operate. Consider the cliché reference to "user friendly" as a means to describe computers: poetry, even the most humane and beautiful, is rarely considered by the masses to be user friendly.

This is not to say that usability is not important. On the contrary, if one cannot understand a creation, this creation certainly cannot allow for a state of mindfulness or encourage creativity. However, in order to realize the state of awareness described above as critical to mindfulness, an element of challenge must be present. The pursuit of a creative solution is not an easy activity, yet the difficulty—the sense of accomplishment that occurs when completing a difficult task—can be thought of as one of the main attractors to participants in the design process. Striking the balance between usability and challenge is a difficult task, one informed by both experience and intuition. The poetics of art begin to clash dramatically with the fundamental need for usability, and future designers will need to make conscious choices of which to give primary importance.

Are people ready for more demanding and poetic experiences? Humanity generally walks a fine line between creativity and consumption. If mindless consumption is thought of as negative, mindful creativity would be the ideal goal of a poetic interaction. This then begs the question: Can our Interaction Design solutions encourage users to be creative?

It is interesting to consider the implications of a design that allows regular people—people who don't claim to be artists and may rarely get a chance to create much of anything at all—to *be creative* and to experience the mindful state of flow described above. Imagine the idea of design empowering regular people to create, and to experience the joy and personal satisfaction that comes with the development of a new idea and the embodiment of that idea in something tangible. Interaction Design that is poetic—honest, mindful, and highly sensory—*can* allow regular people to do just that. An example can be found in the delight one experiences building with LEGO bricks, and this experience has been digitally extended

to include the online LEGO Factory.[74] A regular person, with no design or art training required, can access a website, create a LEGO set using free software provided by LEGO, and can then buy the physical bricks to make his digital creation. The interaction begins to approach the poetic, in that it is honest to the respective medium (digital building as compared to physical building), it demands a sense of mindful play, and is highly visually refined in the traditional brand language of LEGO.

Some practicing designers balk at the idea of designing poetic interactions. One early reviewer of this text was as blunt as to say "I have other things to worry about—like shipping a working product that isn't awful." Yet if designers focus only on the low-hanging fruit of functionalism or usability, the human experience with designed objects is destined to a level of mundane banality. As ideological as it may appear, *what if* that piece of enterprise software offers—for a fleeting moment of use—a poetic experience? A poetic interaction can generally be characterized as having, or encouraging, three main elements: honesty, mindfulness, and a vivid and refined attention to sensory detail. The notion of poetry extends the view of design as communication, building on the view of argument, rhetoric, and design languages. Poetry specifically, and language generally, provides a framework in which to view interactions created through design. These interactions, when properly structured, can afford sensory, emotionally charged, and breathtakingly human experiences.

74 LEGO.
<http://www.lego.com/eng/factory/default.asp>

ON THE NATURE OF INTERACTION AS LANGUAGE

Uday Gajendar

Uday Gajendar is a prolific interaction designer. His work has spanned enterprise software, creative tools, web and tmobile applications, and consumer devices at Oracle, Adobe, Cisco, and Netflix. Uday has also consulted at agencies like frog design and Involution Studios. Holding degrees in both Interaction Design (Carnegie Mellon) and Industrial Design (The University of Michigan), Uday continues to evolve his place within industry, pursuing challenges both wicked and aesthetic. He advances the field with talks and articles about beauty, leadership, and strategy. Further musings about design are posted at his professional blog, http://www.ghostinthepixel.com.

There is no question our landscape of human experience has become over-populated with varieties of artificial (increasingly digital) content, in the form of gadgets, games, services, and even electronically-enhanced fashions, all vying for someone's attention. Some are comparatively primitive (books and pens), while others are more sophisticated (networked healthcare systems). Yet each form is an invitation for a personal encounter to interact and thus play, share, learn, or create, within a specific context—hence, the emergence of situated moments. Each moment involves multiple layers of sense-making and discovery, as the user perceives and interprets the form, functionality, and style—in other words, the design. Questions naturally arise in the user's mind: What is this device for? How do I make it work? What happens if I click this button? The user tries to ascertain the limits and possibilities of the design in question. Thus ensues a tantalizing dialogue between the user and the design towards understanding its meaning and consequence, supporting the user's expectations and goals. What follows is a brief inquiry into this relationship between a user and the "other": a device, service, system, or even the designer.

However, given the overwhelming array of devices and media demanding a user's fractured attention, the issue of creating personal meaning or value becomes paramount as a humanistic concern, increasingly central to design practice, beyond just economic rationale. There is conflict and diversity of interactions that can alienate, frustrate, and annoy as people seek comfort, convenience, and pleasure amid the continuity of their lives—the mundane moments of living like commuting to work, conversing with friends, performing household chores, and taking medications. With this typical "stuff of life," how does one easily make sense of an unfamiliar design, so that it blends into, and enhances, one's lifestyle? Phrased differently, how does a design speak to someone? How does it entice interaction, and the creation of value, thus adding a sense of meaning to one's overall life, beyond the immediacy of that initial moment? Exploring such questions will empower designers with an informed view on ways to best contribute to the enrichment of someone's lifestyle and even the broader cultural condition.

To begin this inquiry, I propose that such value results from well-crafted interactions which shape one's perception of reality, towards something useful, desirable, and meaningful in one's life. It is in the framework of language that an interaction inspires personal relevance ("This object helps me do X every time!") and social significance (social buzz, communities, collaborations). Thus interaction is a generative, constructive phenomenon among a live being, an artificial form, and a context, influencing one's quality of experience, and facilitating the transference (or mutation) of meaning from the designer to the intended user, as mediated by the product's qualities and features.[75] Accordingly, a design is not merely stylish, attention-grabbing ephemera but a vital form of discourse augmenting (or detracting) the cultural (and experiential) landscape in which we live and thrive.

Interaction: Framing the Concept within Design

"We intend to make a highly interactive website…"
—Overheard at a student design presentation

Interaction (and its variants, *interactive* and *interactivity*) has seized public consciousness with the advent and rapid proliferation of the Internet, digital media, broadband networking, mobile devices, video games, and other electronic forms. Indeed, "interactive" has become a loaded marketing buzzword, synonymous with sleek, glamorous hi-tech lifestyles of the "digiterati." If something is labeled as interactive, it is instantly regarded as modern and, supposedly, very marketable. However, as a fundamental concept of human living, interaction has nothing inherently to do with computers. Instead, it is a technologically agnostic concept, with a wide range of applicability: from reading a book, cooking dinner with friends, painting a picture, to drafting budgets and timelines—all which may be augmented with tools and technologies. Indeed, this concept lies at the core of many situations people face in daily life, from science and business to religion and family.

In its purest form *interaction* refers to a dynamic relationship between reciprocating entities at varying types and degrees of influence: people, environment, natural forces, and spiritual/cultural ideals. Obviously, interaction *by itself* has little value and thus needs a framework to enable a useful discussion. User-centered design (UCD) within the domain of human-computer interaction (HCI) provides this organizing element to focus the discussion on design-oriented phenomena. This domain concerns itself primarily with the design of user interfaces, web-based media, mobile devices, and software systems—thus, computer mediated experiences. Design, in this case, means the conception, planning, and making of "the artificial" (products, services, systems, environments) that serve individual and collective human goals. It is a situated activity, dependent upon the circumstances of use (as well as the conditions of product development). It is also a deeply human enterprise, contingent upon personal skills in imagination, empathy, synthetic thinking, and visual communication. The following professional insights further amplify this notion of Design into the realm of interactions:

— A holistic approach including multiple disciplines from computer science, cognitive psychology, sociology, and cultural anthropology, according to Bill Moggridge, co-founder of IDEO design consultancy.

— A multi-sensory continuum consisting of a set of six core elements: control, feedback, productivity, co-creativity, communication, and adaptivity, each on a sliding scale, per Nathan Shedroff's "grand unified theory of information design."

75 Product here refers to graphics, objects, media, services, systems, and environments.

— A profound issue of economic and cultural importance, as it "determines the value of a communication service to its users, and the quality of experience they have when using it," according to Ivrea Interaction Institute co-founder Gillian Crampton-Smith.

So, while we may think of popular expressions of Interaction Design like buttons, links, icons, menus, tabs, on a computer screen, we should consider Herb Simon's scholarly account that "everyone designs who devises courses of action aimed at changing current situations into preferred ones."[76]

Language: passing meaning to others

Language is yet another ambiguous concept for which varieties of theories flourish in the realms of linguistics, cognitive psychology, and sociology. We should note two of many influential contributors to the philosophy of language: Ferdinand Saussure and Ludwig Wittgenstein.

Saussure was a late 19th—early 20th century Swiss linguist; his thinking focused on the formal systemization of signs (for example, icons and buttons). He approached linguistics as a branch of a broader science of signs, which he labeled *semiology* (now *semiotics*). This theory involved signs as the basic unit of a specific language, which he considered as a comprehensive system of signs. As we'll see later, this notion has applicability to design in creating visual iconography systems for graphical interfaces and wayfinding.

Ludwig Wittgenstein was a 20th century Austrian philosopher of language and mind, who helped evolve linguistic theory. Wittgenstein initially prescribed language as pictorial representation of relationships, but later repudiated this, instead advancing the modern notion that the meaning of a word is found in its use in the context of a "language-game." Thus words function and receive their meaning within a context, rather than as atomic, logically predetermined facts or pictures of meaning. For Wittgenstein, the construct of a language game was an "orientation toward action and experience that provided the context for determining meaning."[77] Language is perceived as a human activity, dependent upon the setting of the word used by humans. So, language becomes a shared linguistic practice, which sounds very appropriate to Interaction Design, implying relevant social value.

For our purpose of understanding Interaction Design, we will look at language in terms of situated human use and action. Indeed, we may collectively assume some basic notions at an intuitive level of common use. For example: Language generally refers to that which arises from the systematic integration of utterances, words, or phrases into a regulated pattern of expression, governed by rules for grammar and syntax. Language is a means to facilitate the exchange of information (i.e., communication) from senders to recipients. Ideas, thoughts, emotions, values may be delivered via language. Ultimately, language is about meaning, the creation and delivery of *linguistic* value (more about social and cultural later).

Language, however, is not the same as communication but a necessary precedent. From common observations of politics and advertising we can presume that language is a potent force influencing perceptions of reality.

76   Simon, Herb. *The Sciences of the Artificial*, MIT Press, 3rd Ed. 1996.

77   Dourish, Paul. *Where the Action Is: The Foundations of Embodied Interaction*, MIT Press. 2001.

The sense impression of a word (i.e., connotation) given a cultural context and practical situation can render positive or negative affect of the word upon its reference, impelling certain actions, like voting for a ballot initiative or purchasing one brand of toothpaste over another. Without language there cannot be "actionable" communication that affects one's emotional and linguistic state (i.e., productive debate, etc.). Thus, language is used to identify, qualify, characterize, interpret, and color the phenomena of the world (our reality as we experience and share it). Language is a potent force for designers to comprehend in crafting effective interactions. Of course, a well-rounded review of language requires mention of basic concepts like framing, medium, metaphor, and, the creation of meaning itself.

Metaphors: enabling people to understand

Lakoff and Johnson captivated HCI audiences in the 1970s with their critical work entitled *Metaphors We Live By*, suggesting the primacy of metaphorical thinking in understanding the world's phenomena (i.e., material reality). George Lakoff is a professor of cognitive linguistics, which focuses on the relation between language and underlying mental processes of human cognition in ascertaining reality. According to Lakoff, metaphors, frames, and mappings are necessary interrelated aspects of language's utility in ordinary human correspondence.

Metaphors are "ways of interpreting our daily world with previously experienced and known relationships/associations to enhance meaning, and achieve shared understanding."[78] They are linguistic constructs for seeing one thing in terms of another. But a metaphor is more than just poetic

78   George Lakoff and Johnson. *Metaphors We Live By*. University of Chicago Press, 2nd Ed. 2003.

flourish for embellishment. The human conceptual cognitive system is "fundamentally metaphorical in nature." Indeed metaphors are intrinsically connected to normal human thought patterns, how people conceive and perceive reality, particularly abstractions that require multiple metaphors for maximum understanding. So, metaphors are basically conceptual aids to understand abstract entities in terms of concrete objects, thus helping people make sense of the complex, dynamic surroundings. Much of this is predicated upon the "embodied mind" notion of human bodies (and almost symbiotically connected mind) having physical experiences in a spatial orientation, which affects the perception of reality accordingly from that viewpoint. Two digital examples enforce this.

The most popular computer metaphor is the desktop GUI (graphical user interface) model of interaction, with files, folders, windows, and even a trashcan; this model makes a visual computing environment more comprehensible and accessible to office workers by relating it to real-world references in the office space, to some degree of fidelity.

Another metaphor commonly used for enterprise software is the "dashboard" interface for showing multiple status indicators and performance metrics constantly updated in real-time within compartmentalized visual regions, much like an automobile's dashboard: speedometer, odometer, fuel gauge, etc. This enables better sense-making of complex data, by making it seem like a more familiar form.

Thus, a metaphor operates through a mapping of conceptual domains, to facilitate the interpretation of the unfamiliar in terms of the familiar. In so doing there is attribution of values, behaviors, and styles from the concrete to abstract, (and vice versa) to ensure appropriateness of fit by the participant. Again, the example of the desktop GUI comes to light as a more human recognition of what is essentially 1's and 0's, or basic machine code. In some cases the metaphor "breaks" due to faulty mapping. Indeed, this is often the case for mismatched affordances of a design: mapping cues don't fit the user's expected sense of how a design should behave. Referring back to the desktop interface, the notion of "minimizing windows" or "folder directories" somewhat breaks from the actual real-world references of file cabinets and tabletops.

Finally, the notion of frame figures into Lakoff's theory of metaphors in that frames set the overall perspective to help shape the meaning of a given linguistic concept. This is commonly seen in political rhetoric, with the "spinning" of controversial issues towards a specific advantage, by framing the debate using certain wording favorable to the intended listener. For example, politicians may frame the hot issue of taxation by using the words "relief" or "breaks" to suggest taxation is an adversity or pain to be relieved from.

In the world of Interaction Design, the use of mice and keyboards frames the model of interaction with visual computing environments. This hardware sets the assumption of drag-and-drop, point-and-click, type to enter values, and right-click to trigger a context menu, aptly drawing a certain kind of discourse with the GUI. Another example, the new Xbox360 gaming system, uses the phrase "Ring of Light" instead of "Power Button" to romanticize the mere act of turning on the next-generation gaming unit. Microsoft's Windows XP uses a visually embellished "Start" button to convey that is the starting point for a journey of digital encounters, framing computer use as more than just a series of tedious computational tasks. And, for that matter, Apple's use of the "Happy Mac face" (half computer/half human) and uplifting "dial tone" upon starting up the very first Macintosh established a very human sense—far more inviting than a blinking text cursor!

Affordances: Interaction and Language in Practice

The concepts of interaction and language are tantalizingly close in achieving a useful relationship for designers in their daily practice. For an interaction to make sense, it needs a language to communicate. For language to express meaning, that meaning is found in the interaction of parts with a cognitively alert, live being, along with a full sense of expectations and cultural or social values of the immediate situation. These concepts go hand-in-hand by necessity; one cannot exist without the other.

This reflexive relationship becomes more evident by looking at the affordances and constraints upon interaction of everyday real objects. Through affordances a design speaks to users, provoking or inviting an encounter to ensue. Its level of success depends on the clarity, appropriateness, and conceptual linkage of the affordance to user's goals and expectations.

Affordance has gained popularity in HCI circles, primarily through Donald Norman's thoughtful analysis of the usability of everyday objects (chairs, doors, thermostats, tea kettles). *Affordance* refers to the "property of an environment that supports action to appropriately equipped organisms."[79] For example, a chair's typical L-shaped structure affords people sitting (since an able-bodied person can naturally bend legs and torso easily), while a door's knob affords turning to open (since I have the requisite functional hands to turn the knob—for a person whose hands are

79   Dourish, Paul. *Where the Action Is: The Foundations of Embodied Interaction*, MIT Press. 2001.

full of grocery bags, however, the knobs are a hindrance). Going further, affordance, according to HCI scholar Paul Dourish, is a triadic relation among *environment*, *organism*, and *activity* focused on the notion of "being in the world," acting in embodied space to accomplish some goal.[80] Affordances are a form of communication, telling the user what is possible with a design—and constraining him to that possibility by virtue of materials, mechanics, and so forth.

Consider the shift in PDA (Personal digital assistant) devices from Apple's pioneering Newton to recent models from HP and Palm. These devices feature a stylus for pen-based interaction, resembling the natural feel of writing and gesturing with a pen. The device and screen afford tapping, writing, drawing, all the expected motions of pen-based manipulation, aligning with the intended metaphor of a portable digital notepad that frames the interactive encounter. However, the PDA software constrains the writing to a specific symbol lexicon (Graffiti), to approximate handwriting recognition.

A web-based business application (like Oracle Financials or SAP Supply Chain) conveys its affordances via consistent visual interactive elements: icons, buttons, links, tabs, menus, and various states thereof (hover, depressed, unselected, disabled, etc.). However, it's often not quite clear initially how various affordances relate to content and functionality, or the user's tasks—hence the challenge of virtual information spaces, with potentially N-layers deep of data and navigation. Site maps and directories provide some guidance. But through prior familiarity with standard web widgets, users armed with a mouse know that a dropdown list affords click and scroll to select a choice. Similarly, tabs have come to mean compartmentalized regions of content/functionality to be clicked to access that area.

BMW's iDrive is arguably the most ambitious attempt at mapping literally hundreds of possible actions and modes to a single control whose one affordance is turning and clicking a dial—while operating a two-ton vehicle at high speeds or in congested traffic. The invisibility of relationship between form and function (and the user's attempt to decipher it while driving) contributes to the high frustration and poor usability.

Such examples suggest how meaning arises in the use of the product, by virtue of understanding the affordances, constraints, and mappings of form and functionality. User interaction occurs in a particular manner as constrained by the materials and mechanics of the form and features, which should be visibly mapped to user's model of expected behavior, with real-time apprehension of consequence and feedback. Thus the user can modify her actions accordingly to achieve the optimal expected result: listening to music, jotting down notes, submitting financial reports, or adjusting the temperature.

Design as communication: the essential theme revealed

The intersection of the core concepts—interaction and language—suggests the idea of design as an overarching platform for communication, the exchange of information from sender to receiver given a certain context. Indeed, the act of designing a product is a socially communicative act, of delivering value to an intended target audience, so as to evoke some

---

80   Dourish, Paul. *Where the Action Is: The Foundations of Embodied Interaction.* MIT Press, 2004.

response—emotional, physical, psychological, even social. On various levels communication can be regarded as a method of argument, grammar of symbols, or projection of sense/value upon the world.

Rhetorical meaning

Design scholars Richard Buchanan and Victor Margolin have proposed a rhetorical approach to design, as a humanistic activity dedicated to productive inquiry and making. Thus, it is an architectonic art, a systematic integrative discipline of forethought, a master art of strategic thinking that organizes and structures patterns of thought into new and powerful ways; narrative and argument are core aspects. Rhetoric is concerned with discovery, invention, argument, and planning. At its heart is the issue of persuasive communication, in which each designed entity embodies a well- formed argument. This view of the product as an argument suggests that the designer is like a speaker composing a speech, to be delivered to a specific audience. A product design is a situated act, relying upon balanced, nuanced relations known informally as the "Rhetorical Stance," from rhetorician Wayne Booth.[81] Only through interdependence of the Classical elements (logos, ethos, pathos) can a speech be effective. Balance is found when it can change minds. An overemphasis on logos, ethos, or pathos will result in awkward, unnatural performance that does not achieve its goal of audience persuasion (i.e., move the user to favorable action). This argument is comprised of specific parts (drawn from Classical concepts initially outlined by Aristotle, Cicero, and other rhetorical thinkers), that should be held in balance: the logical structure of rational components (*logos*), human

affordances and ergonomic qualities to ensure value (*pathos*), and a tone of voice or style (*ethos*). Rounding out is another aspect of narrative, or *mythos*, that conveys a unifying sense of story or plot structure for how the object fits the user's scenario.[82]

Interpretations of signs

Briefly discussed earlier, semiotics was first conceived as a science of signs and symbols for communicative purpose. Semiotics explains the principles that underlie the structure of signs and their utility within messages. Valuing semiotics helps designers decide how to select and arrange the elements that comprise the message (buttons, links, icons, animations, etc.). Recent scholars suggest that a sign is the result of a signing process (known as *semiosis*), involving a balanced relationship among three critical elements: the *signifier* (which is some representation of an object, like an icon or symbol or image), the *signified* (the object which is being represented visually), and the *interpretant* (the human being interpreting the relationship of signifier and signified, imbued with his own set of social, cultural, and experiential background in the deciphering).

Mullet and Sano, authors of *Designing Visual Interfaces*, explore this in-depth with tangible examples, geared towards communications for screen-based computing environments. By clearly discussing atomic, essential principles, (like clarity, restraint, hierarchy, balance), they provide basic heuristics on effective visual communication techniques that designers can apply to develop their own sense of visual language for a given situation.

81 Booth, Wayne. *The Essential Wayne Booth*. University of Chicago Press, 2006.

82 Buchanan, Richard. "Declaration by Design: Rhetoric, Argument, and Demonstration in Design Practice." Design Discourse: History, Theory, Criticism. Ed Victor Margolin. The University of Chicago Press, 1989

Taking this approach, then, suggests that meaning is heavily dependent on the notion of interpretation, as a process of "reconstructing the meaning of a sign by identifying the sign object and grasping the significance of the connection."[83] From this view, meaning comes from a person's interpretation of signs.

Complex financial business applications (accounting, cash management, taxation) have several hundred visual icons of varying subtleties of distinction, given the different mode or functional area of the application. Interpretation will vary per user type, task setting, goal, and expectations of the user. Some icons are clickable, others are status only indicators. In interaction and usage, the user will learn the differences.

The Xbox 360 game controller has a pre-set layout of buttons, marked with letters and in primary colors (red, blue, green, yellow) whose meanings vary per game—sometimes within the different stages of a game itself, depending on player mode (in EA Sports' NFL Madden 2006 Football, the modes change depending on whether a player is passing, kicking, running, or tackling). There is a mapping of the symbol on the gamepad to the virtual player capabilities, shown on the game screen.

Making Meaning

HCI scholar/scientist Paul Dourish has hypothesized a different take on Interaction Design, that he terms as "embodied interaction," a new model of interpreting interaction that extends recent HCI research trends in "tangible" and "social" computing.[84] Dourish's argument is based upon the philosophical framework of *phenomenology* which is the study of experience and existence, that are intuitively felt and known by factual presence in the world. Dourish contends that embodiment is more than a physical property but is about social presence and participatory status in the world, having an (inter) active role in changing and becoming. Everyday engagement in daily activities and task completion is another core tenet; the setting of action defines the value and manner of the action. Thus meaning emerges from the participation of an individual agent with some object within a setting—a constant negotiation or conversation unfolding. It is formed continuously and interactively, in real-time action/location; meaning is *not* simply projected or found but instead created and shared through engagement with the artificial.[85] This is a profound view of interaction that shifts the emphasis from the designer crafting the argument, or the interpretation of images, towards the place of action between the user and the object in question, given a situation *and* the particular lifestyle of the user.

This view encourages the designer to regard design as a participatory activity, not simply dictating to the user, but allowing the user to evolve and shape the encounter so it is a co-creative opportunity. Indeed, this view presupposes that the user can manipulate or improvise the design to suit her needs at the moment, as recently suggested by IDEO designer Janet Fulton Suri, in her account of everyday actions, *Thoughtless Acts*. Suri's work explores what occurs when ordinary objects are re-cast for impromptu purposes—for example, using your suitcase as a seat at an airport internet kiosk.

83 Ibid.

84 Dourish, Paul. Where the Action Is: *The Foundations of Embodied Interaction.* The MIT Press, 2004.

85 Ibid.

Another example to consider: Videogame interaction is a highly complex form of communication and engagement, whose meaning arises from the immediate, real-time encounter between the player, the controller, the game console, and the video imagery on the TV display. There is a coalescence of game play, game mechanics, and game interface that constitute the total value of the interaction, its meaning in terms of responsiveness of game interactivity and how it fits within situation/context of leisurely activity. There is learning, pleasure, frustration, and overall struggle and resolution in that continuous, unfolding moment of participation.

Thus, in summary, through the intersection of interaction and language, design becomes a platform for communication. Viable, actionable communication can occur from a variety of viewpoints: rhetorical, semiotic, or phenomenal. There are certainly others but these specific views sufficiently capture key issues of influence, interpretation, and engagement that characterize an interaction. In guiding the designer who seeks an effective communication-oriented solution, these views parcel out finer issues for debate and iteration. These are simply ways to perceive how meaning comes to be in interaction, when regarded as a communicative activity. In actual practice, however, an interactive encounter (and thus meaning itself) combines all three views into a dynamic, self-sufficient, whole user experience.

We have taken a path through the nexus of interaction and language to understand how to create products that deliver positive value to users, and thereby implicitly suggest a broader cultural backdrop of experience. Interaction shapes the perception of reality. A coherent and consistent system of interactions within the framework of design suggests a language of relationship building between people (user + designer, user + other users)

mediated by the designed artifice. Value and meaning are deliberated, interpreted, and created via the interactive encounter, at multiple levels: emotional, cognitive, physical, visual. This activity (construed as a conversation or dialogue) characterizes the user experience of an artifact, which can proliferate and aggregate to impact society and culture at large, shaping values, norms, beliefs, attitudes, expectations, or standards of what is acceptable or appropriate. One's way of life or lifestyle itself can be influenced by well-informed Interaction Designs, to yield a satisfying, memorable quality of experience—one that can be shared, repeated, and enhanced.

SECTION FOUR

CHALLENGES FACING
INTERACTION DESIGN IN INDUSTRY

4

Interaction Design is slowly gaining recognition in industry, finding a strategic home between marketing and engineering. Interaction Designers are placed in teams at high-tech companies like Google and Yahoo, and also have become established as contributors in small consultancies like IDEO or Ziba. Yet while Interaction Design continues to creep into enterprises big and small, many Interaction Designers remain pessimistic regarding their ability to effect positive change in the development of products. Interaction Designers continually discuss career problems relating to organizational respect, use (or lack thereof) of methodology, ambiguity of job description, and project ownership. These problems may be due to the relative "newness" of Interaction Design as a profession. As the profession has grown and proven itself, project teams have begun to trust Interaction Designers with more responsibility. At the same time, however, the difficulty in identifying the outcome of Interaction Design efforts makes this a difficult profession to explain. Development teams realize they need Interaction Design, but they aren't necessarily sure why. Additionally, the ambiguity of the end creation makes it difficult for Interaction Designers to find a home in the traditional structure of many corporations or consultancies. A designer is neither an engineer, programmer, or scientist, nor a writer, artist, or stylist. Of course, paradoxically, a good Interaction Designer is a bit of all of these things. In order to claim the respect necessary to rise to a decision-making position, the community of Interaction Designers needs to better educate the business world about what Interaction Design is, what it does, and why it is important. This education requires a great deal of passion and patience, and some sort of central organizational body and framework.

CHAPTER SEVEN:
THE POLITICAL DYNAMICS OF PRODUCT DEVELOPMENT

The fight for "ownership" during the development of a product—either physical or digital—is not a new fight. There has long existed tension between management, engineering, and "creative" over who should be responsible for the leadership and vision required to bring a product to fruition. The project manager, overwhelmed with criteria from various stakeholders, is usually responsible for the development of a specification document known as a "spec" (or project document). This written bible for development becomes the ultimate check against functionality, features, cost, and timeframe in which to bring a product to market. The content of the "spec" traditionally balances issues of quality engineering, competitive guidelines, brand analysis, and detailed design features, and one can imagine that such a document is both hard to write and hard to read in any manageable time frame. In many companies, the project manager becomes, in some respect, the "advocate for the spec." Debate or criticism of content in a piece of hardware or software is quickly squelched because "it's not in the spec."

While the stereotypical project manager is consumed by problems of feature creep and budget allocation, the engineer speaks softly but carries a much bigger stick: The engineer is the individual responsible for actually implementing things and it is frequently the engineer who gets final say over the completeness of a product. This is particularly common in companies run and owned by other engineers, which is quite normal in the tech sector. A not very funny joke in the world of engineering regards issues of quality, cost, and completion. The engineer says to the project manager, "You can have the product working, under budget, or completed on time—pick only two." The various flavors of this platitude imply a particularly large gap in understanding between cultures of management and cultures of development. The engineer realizes the realities of development include unforeseen circumstances and problems to be solved along the way. A mediocre manager learns to ignore all problems found outside the realm of the specifications document. The spec dictates function, cost, and time—just follow the spec, and all will emerge in one piece.

There is also another member of the development team vying for leadership in the development of a product: the marketer. The marketer has traditionally been thought of as a form of salesman. Marketing was used to create advertising campaigns to move products externally. Many companies have seen a shift away from traditional advertising, in an effort to capitalize on new technologies, and there has increasingly been an introduction of words like "rogue" or "guerilla" associated with marketing techniques. Perhaps this shift is due to the realization that marketing as a brute force "campaign" to encourage and promote sales might not work. Commercials are frequently ignored, and the consumer has learned to block out the constant barrage of product placement in popular films and television shows. Marketers understand that technology provides new opportunities to move product, but technological advances in marketing usually mean more intrusive and obnoxious ways to advertise. In response, a new breed of marketers has emerged. Educated in the early 1990s, this group is frequently referred to as the "creative" department and include those with MBA degrees. Commonly, these MBAs find their way into positions of marketing *management*. Recently, and particularly in high-tech companies, this marketing management position translates into a strange combination of the external salesmanship described above and a form of internal governance and ownership. These marketers are trained in formal business practices and gravitate towards the creation of a spec with a fancier name (the PRD, or Product Requirement Document) and fancier graphics. The "creative group" is usually considered both client present-able and user presentable. These marketers have probably discussed the development initiative with various stakeholders (either internally or externally), and they may have even conducted some focus groups with users to determine what they think they want out of a new product.

Unfortunately, this bizarre combination of roles (marketer as external publicity engine and internal project leader) doesn't adequately address many of the new and complicated challenges modern businesses face with regard to technology, shrinking price points and offshore product development. Specifically, thoughts of "campaign-style" marketing leave little room for the necessary duality of convergent and divergent strategy. A business problem is no longer a linear path from invention to production to distribution. Instead, the development of a product requires the strategic analysis of conceptual and historical frameworks of ideas, the mapping of complicated data, and a highly emotionally-charged understanding of humanity and human needs.

Interaction Design at the center of the world

Thus, there end up a diverse assortment of players vying for internal ownership, rather than a collaborative team participating in a cohesive strategy for success. Strategy implies an elaborate plan for accomplishing something, and business relies on strategic imperatives to drive a company in a certain direction. Strategy is usually considered long term and broad. A strategic approach is usually complicated, multi-tiered, and process centered. These are all qualities of an Interaction Design process, too. Bernie Marcus and Arthur Blank, founders of The Home Depot, reflect on the importance of strategic relationships that value people: "We had customers coming into our stores who were consumers of many of these [manufacturer's] products. When they couldn't buy these products in our stores, they bought something else. So we had to convince the manufac-turers that they had to be in our stores because that's where their custom-ers were. That was our selling point… Every business is there to please the customer."[86] Again, the general trend of strategic business success is customer focused. While a primary tenet of any business is to make a profit, a more fundamental goal should be to "understand humanity."

As has been previously discussed, Interaction Designers are in the business of understanding people in order to act as their advocate. Yet curricula in business administration or economic theory generally do not focus on the individual: Emphasis placed on humanity usually highlights the group (market behavior, demographics, etc.) instead. Few marketers or executives have been formally trained in issues of design or psychology, much less anthropology or sociology.

Interaction Designers have a similar problem to overcome: They haven't been trained in issues of business. How critical is that formal busi-ness training in preparing one for the pragmatic strain of business admin-istration? According to Tom Peters, not very. As he recollects some twenty years after writing *In Search of Excellence*, Peters relates a particularly relevant anecdote of John Young, the president of Hewlett-Packard, sitting in a common cubicle and wearing shirtsleeves. In order to truly understand how to manage his people, Young immersed himself in the environment of work—he became one of the regular workers, and led his team by becom-

86 Marcus, Bernie, et al. *Built from Scratch: How a Couple of Regular Guys Grew the Home Depot from Nothing to $30 Billion.* Crown Business, 1999.

ing the team.[87] The informal approach to management may ultimately work better than more traditional management techniques in shepherding the creative process of Interaction Design.

The following contribution is written by a practicing Interaction Designer who has experienced the unique relationship Interaction Design has with the rest of the business and engineering community. Interaction Designer Ellen Beldner offers her thoughts on communicating with product and project managers in the course of the development of software. She articulates the value Interaction Design can provide to a project team, and uses her own experiences at Google to illustrate some of the challenges—and ways around these challenges—Interaction Designers face in industry.

87   Tom Peter's True Confessions. Fast Company, December, 2001.
<http://www.fastcompany.com/magazine/53/peters.html>

GETTING DESIGN DONE

Ellen Beldner, ChoiceVendor

Ellen Beldner is the User Experience director at ChoiceVendor, a business software startup in San Francisco. She has been designing software in Silicon Valley since 2000, including four years as a UE designer at Google (when this essay was originally written) and a year leading the design of YouTube's monetization and copyright-monitoring software. Ellen graduated from Carnegie Mellon University with a degree in HCI and professional writing, and her focus is on enterprise and expert-use software.

Designers make decisions. We must make them in the face of uncertainty, of constraints imposed by medium, time, and fiat, constantly balancing immensely complex systems of interwoven attributes and elements. But the designer is *a* person—not *the* person—who makes decisions. Designers must learn not just how to make decisions about the interface, but how to navigate group decision-making processes with an essential design vision left intact.

Additionally, designers communicate. One of the biggest lessons I have learned about the practice of design is that it takes at least as much time to communicate your design to other people as it does to generate and plan the solution.

We also communicate to help our teams make non-UI decisions. Visualizations like flowcharts force the team to think about where the accounting system kicks in and where they have to get inventory to talk to shipping—even though they're writing the credit card processor and those other systems weren't obviously part of the payment mechanism. These are

not interface decisions and the designer does not own them, but our skills as communicators, sketchers, and documenters make this an important secondary role.

Cooper[88] finds the communication role sufficiently important and time-consuming that it hires design communicators, saying in the online job description, "[i]f our vision is to be realized, it is essential that we effectively communicate the design and its rationale."[89] The role is particularly important at a consultancy, where much of the project's value is projected through its deliverables. I once attended a talk given by a designer from Meta. He showed one of their gorgeous 11x17 color-printed design deliverable books. The book was bound and must have been 200 pages. It was impressive, and documented the output of a million-dollar branding and site design project for a startup created around 1999. He told us that they spent a huge amount of time designing and producing that deliverable, because as a consultancy working on such massively expensive projects, they learned that clients want something physical to hold on to. They needed a physical artifact to embody the value of the design work that had been done.

Designers are familiar with the rule of sketchification: don't make your prototypes look too fancy or polished, or you'll never get really challenging feedback. Your clients, team, and users will hesitate to rip apart something that is too finished. Showing people deliberately sloppy

---

88   The design shop formerly known as "Cooper Interaction Design." Naming the firm with the same word that is used to refer to its founder and principal, Alan Cooper, strikes me as a bit confusing due to ambiguity of referent. There is not a chance that this ambiguity slipped by unnoticed. I wonder: what direction does the metonymy go?

89   http://www.cooper.com/content/company/design_communicator.asp.

sketch work in early-stage design ensures that you gain very high-level feedback. We forget, however, the converse: when you produce polished and thorough deliverables, you help encapsulate product decisions and give yourself and the team a sense of making decisions and having learned and progressed. Spend some time producing a few landmark deliverables on each project. They'll serve as reference points for you and the rest of the team.

Many teams and projects don't think to ask designers for deliverables not immediately related to the UI, be it early sketchwork or auxiliary flow charts to help a team figure out what it's doing. On every project that I've used these rapid prototyping techniques and IA-style low-fidelity deliverables, even without initial support, team leads have thanked me. Most engineering managers notice the difference and have specifically requested that my colleagues do more of this work. The work named "Information Architecture," pretentious as it sounds to many engineers and managers, specifically prevents many of the horrors that design-by-VP and design-by-committee unleash on the world.

I get a sort of perverse satisfaction when engineers, totally innocent of any design methodology prejudices, come out of design-by-committee meeting shell shocked and horrified. "Is this what you do?" they ask me. "Why is getting a good UI such a painful experience?" I explain that it doesn't have to be that bad, and in fact, that design-by-committee is known in the field to be extremely painful and time-consuming. The stuff that many managers reject as nonsense—IA, flow diagrams, user story flows—actually makes life better.

I was on a major project several years ago where the product manager didn't realize the value of IA work; the tech lead thought it was silly, and I was too green to firmly stand up for the process by doing the work and demonstrating its value. As a result, we had a nightmare of a process with 6 months of daily UI review meetings in which every minute decision got revisited a thousand times and the resulting UI was confused and fairly incoherent. Not to mention the effect on team morale—two junior PMs, the UI engineer, the usability analyst, and I were miserable on that project. I suspect that the only two people who got anything out of it were the senior PM and the tech lead, who ended up dating for two years afterwards.

Good, non-bureaucratic IA work helps scope and structure decisions, and it tends to remove dependencies on having an entire UI done before engineering can start (referred to, generally with shudders, as "waterfall design"). Begin with use cases and scenarios: make decisions about what the product needs to let people do—and you get the team to agree on that part. From there, it tends to be easier to figure out what features make sense and what features are most important, and you typically get reasonable agreement on what features are needed first and which ones are nice-to-haves. Engineering can start architecting the major systems needed. Then, given the feature set, you can start planning the particular pages and interface widgets that will support those features.

This means that you will have less control over the total system but that the system will get launched faster. As you're working out the details of the design you may realize that you want, say, the rate of change in duration between user logins to drive the appearance of a help tip. The engineers tell you that it would take a massive database restructure. Had you completely designed the system before any engineering work took place and written a full UI spec, yes, the engineers would have known the requirement and could have built it into the system: but then engineering work would have been delayed by a few months.

Where the designer's word is law—or where there is an interfering VP or a scatterbrained PM—late feature revelations are disastrous. The HCI field has strenuously proven in the last 25 years that it's worth the engineering time to generally have high-level design researched and completed before engineering work begins. But in practice, particularly at software companies, the detailed subtleties of interface design are very rarely reason to restructure the database or hold back on launch. And even though product planning typically begins before significant engineering expenditure, the people who do the product planning are very rarely people who are trained in user-centered product design. Designers are often seen as more of an engineering resource: someone to call in when you start to build, not when you start to plan.

So over time you learn to anticipate the needs of your team and your product: by the time they ask for the feature, you already have a fully done design spec that is backed by usability work. The fact that the work is already done and tested is a good enough reason, in most of these fast-paced no-time-to-think situations, to follow the design.

Don't let anyone force you into particular mechanisms of design, be it a process or deliverable. All of these artifacts, all of these processes and methodologies exist because different people figured out what it takes to get design work delivered. Clever anthropologists and PhD HCI students distilled lots of these techniques, boiled them down into one process or another, and those processes folded back into the field.

Thus we all know that you start with needs and requirements gathering, do iterative prototyping based on team and usability feedback, and then develop and deploy.

Except Google.[90]

It always shocks practitioners from school or other companies when I mention that most of Google's product design and development is nothing like the practice we're taught about in school—yet it gets the job done. Decisions are scrutinized from the highest level. Product managers are generally instructed that they own the user interface. Early stage field research is regarded with a solid dose of skepticism and is underutilized by PMs and tech leads who aren't trained to inform product decisions with it. In most cases, we design and build some level of prototype, and then a designer is called in: either a face-lifted product gets launched and then we do usability and start revising it to task-centricness; or we do task-centricness and it gets launched as an alpha or beta.

I find it problematic to categorically say that the interaction designer is the arbiter of all interaction and must be ultimately responsible for the user experience of a product, working with a phalanx of graphic designers, interface programmers, usability analysts, and the like. This is because lots of good products get made without someone who is a trained and practicing designer. I would love to bestow automatic and official authority on anyone who does meet the qualifications of a designer, but that's as silly as saying that only the person who graduated from culinary school should be

---

90   And maybe Apple, although I haven't worked there so I don't know - I just hear rumors.

roasting the chicken. Roasting a chicken isn't as easy as making toast, but if you follow directions you'll be fine. In reality, chickens get roasted and product decisions get made by all sorts of people for all sorts of reasons.[91]

If you are trained in the science of Human-Computer Interaction and in the art of design; if you are intuitive and emotive and empathetic; if you are logical and creative, artistic and mathematical; you are a designer *and you need to be calling the shots*. It makes sense. It is why you were hired. You have the right to the authority of your expertise. Sure, you will mess up and make bad decisions on occasion, and being the designer does not mean you are a prima-donna who is allowed to ignore feedback. But the person who has the most expertise in user-centered design (you, presumably) should be the one who bears the responsibility for design decisions. It's maximizing efficiency on your team.[92]

Most people who study HCI or one of the design fields go into that field in the first place because they want to design products start to finish. Designers are taught processes and procedures for working with bizdev people and with engineers and marketing and writing; for doing early UI prototyping that can be tested, in order to make decisions without all the drama; for gathering requirements that are based on fact and vision; for staging decisions appropriately; and for validating and testing assumptions in a timely way. This isn't all that is needed to launch a product and I don't want to insinuate that the world's problems would be solved if only UI were in charge of everything. But you must seize decision space where you are the expert, and consequently you must take responsibility for the mistakes you will make.

Working with product managers

When I was preparing to quit a previous job, I made an outline of the reasons I wanted to quit, as a prelude to my exit interview. The list began like this:

1. Had to instruct "Vince," my product manager, to stop touching me ("Don't worry. You'll have your say." [pat pat pat])
a. My product manager has a bald spot, is short, drives a Camaro, and smells like garlic.
i. I know what my product manager smells like
2. I am being explicitly told to plagiarize the UI for our competitor's analogous product.
a. That software is a failed product made by a company that just got de-listed from the stock exchange. The goal of their recent redesign—for which they had paid frog design a well-deserved several million—was widget-level consistency amongst all the products in that company's massive product suite. But that product, just like their others, was not designed for the task at hand in a user-centric way.

---

91 On the other hand, if you have Jamie Oliver or Dana Stewart standing behind you, apron on, waving a pepper grinder and a bowl of cornbread stuffing, saying "Would you please get out of the kitchen so I can cook you an awesome chicken? Please? Seriously. You're pissing me off. Don't you want a yummy chicken? I'd really love to make one for you. It's my special recipe," you'd get out of the way, wouldn't you?

92 Not only is it really slow to have a team of 8 people making collaborative decisions on tiny UI details, but it makes you want to poke out each other's eyeballs. Missing eyeballs are not good for team morale; if there is one thing Kill Bill taught me, it's that.

3. Vince micromanages the UI and tells me to do things that contradict 20 years of HCI research with no reason other than "Our competitors do it." I have expressed my frustration at this situation to him and to my manager, to no avail.[93]

I quit that job because the product manager was a micromanager who didn't know what he was doing. He took no pride in designing the best software possible; he was unwilling to listen to or consider my expertise; and he told me to do things that I thought were professionally unethical. Most designers work in these conditions every day. At Google, there is one PM that many of us work with at some point or another—let's call him Richard. He has quite a lot of jurisdiction. There's a point about 3 or 6 months into each designer's stint when they start to get sort of quiet and flummoxed… and then there's the fateful day when they come back from a meeting with a glazed look in their eye. They cautiously approach a designer who's been around longer and say "So…. I was wondering… I just got back from this review…."

The designer who's been there longer nods their head and says "come with me." You take the newer designer—and these are not novices; they have come from Stanford, CMU, Berkeley; Ebay, Amazon, Microsoft—into a conference room and you say:

"Richard's UI review meeting?"

Their eyes light up: you understand.

"Yeah… is it…?"

"Always like that? Yes."

We had one designer on staff: experienced and talented, who had started from one of our more successful acquisitions. He went into a review one day with bullet points on each search result. Richard asked, "Why are you using bullet points? Those are too heavy on the page—could you try hyphens and come back next week?"

So that designer not only did mockups with hyphens, but with plusses, no punctuation, and quite a few other variants. The next week, I was sitting at my desk when he returned to the cubes, shaking his head with a look of peeved astonishment on his face, lip curled, eyebrows raised, mouth slightly agape in that "WTF" expression.

"What happened?" I asked.

"Richard took one look at the blurbs, with all the variants I had done, stopped me mid-sentence, and said, 'why aren't you using bullets?'"

"You're kidding me."

"Nope. Screw this. I'm just gonna keep doing what he tells me until he shuts up." That designer quit not long after.

I've looked for information on the profession of product management. It is not a formalized or academic field: it's a position that exists only within industry. There is very little professional literature about what it means to be a product manager—much less a good one. The field of HCI has spent the past 20 years yelling its head off about how to work with

---

93   The list continued with some choice remarks about the intelligence of the CEO and the motivational posters on the walls. No joke, I walked in one day before a potential client toured the office as part of a due diligence check and found "Teamwork: When we all work together, we all win together" and "Flexibility: stretch your potential."

engineers; as a result, most engineers are comfortable and happy with basic user-centric methodologies (like prototyping before implementation and doing user testing to help make decisions faster).

Yet no one teaches product managers how to do their job. This is not to say that PMs do not serve a function or are incompetent at greater rates than the general population. From what I have seen, the PM's role tends to deal with business requirements, UI themes and flows, and prioritizing technical work and features. Clearly PMs serve useful functions and do useful things, or companies like Microsoft, Google, and all the other major software development organizations wouldn't have so many people filling this role. And I've worked with PMs who I completely love; I wouldn't trade their presence on projects for anything. I usually find those engagements successful because our skills are complementary. They do work that is unique to their expertise and I do work that is unique to mine. Everyone feels like a useful and valued contributor.

Now that I work at a company with a large design staff and even more product managers, I can see how each of us works well with different product managers. Jill is a super-organized checklist-driven micromanaging machine: I go nuts when I work with her because if I'm missing one mockup or go in a direction she didn't expect, she gets upset. Other designers think this is dandy. I like working with Peter because he's chaotic and it gives me a lot of space to define the UI and decide what we need to do, but this makes some designers bonkers because they're not interested in the project planning aspects.

Working relationships can be every bit as dysfunctional and demoralizing as romantic relationships. Finding a job that you love is at least as hard as finding a great partner—harder, perhaps, because it's like dating the 5 or 6 people on the immediate team rather than just the one boyfriend.

Over time you learn to quickly identify the sorts of projects that will be a breeze and the ones that will test your skills. Be conscious and deliberate about this. Keep notes about what makes you the happiest when you're working, and where you drag your feet. When you interview for new jobs or move on to new projects, you'll get better and better at matching yourself to situations where you're doing what you want—and at least you'll have more accurate expectations going in.

Your job is to make decisions and deliver them to other people.

Design is deliberate decision-making—which is sometimes ruthless—in pursuit of a vision.

Design is rhetoric. It is the act of communicating an idea to a particular audience, generally using a particular medium.

And it is the job of the interaction designer to make decisions about the product and its interface and then communicate those decisions to the people who have to build the product.[94]

----

94   This is like Sen-Rikyu, the father of the modern Japanese tea ceremony, explaining this ceremony as follows: "Tea is naught but this. First you make the water boil. Then infuse the tea. Then you drink it properly. That is all you need to know."

One of the greatest blocks to good design is the tension between authoritative decision-making and the humility and creativity that are at the core of our profession. You cannot be a good designer or engineer unless you are always trying to solve problems amidst new constraints.[95]

Moreover, it is inimical to your nature as a designer to not allow yourself the hubris of too much authoritativeness. You know for a fact—you must know—that at any point your design may be proven ineffective for its purported uses. No matter how much you believe in the design, if it doesn't work, you have to let it go.

So we often find ourselves hesitant to make authoritative recommendations. An engineer or PM can justifiably say "well, but what about this use case? It would suggest that we make the flow work like *this*, instead." You can get stymied, circling back and forth between designs, unable to make a decision or preserve a coherent vision of the interface.

You must learn to make decisions in the face of uncertainty, always preserving your memory of the paths and solutions you did not happen to take so you can return if you need to revisit a decision. Designers always have to make decisions with imperfect data, and very often with inadequate data. When you can't make authoritative decisions because you don't have sufficient data, you have to state assumptions and make recommendations.

When you aren't sure, proactively point it out to your teammates. Bring it up for discussion and collect their feedback: one of them may have some additional data or insight. Point out the weaknesses in your own work and the gaps in your knowledge; it will mitigate risk for the project. You should also suggest a plan for what type of data you'd need to make that decision; if you work with a usability analyst, he may have better suggestions, and he'll definitely know how to get the data that you need. Engineers may be able to collect data or run a logs analysis; your PM might be able to set up a focus group.

Given the methodological squishiness of most fieldwork and usability testing, your data will never be perfectly reliable. Some data, however, is better than none. Even if you're reading a collection of interviews from CIO magazine about average costs of enterprise software installations, you will have some objective, external thing to point to and say "this is why we're going to do it this way. We may be wrong, but we'll make a note of this as an assumption to keep an eye on over time."

Jack of all trades, master of none

If you have 2 years in the field versus 10 versus 20, you will have widely different competence at managing projects and making good decisions. And as you negotiate your role on a particular project, you will have to draw boundaries between yourself and the tech lead, yourself and the product manager.

I think many designers have a tendency to take on more than our capacities truly allow. First, you're afraid to say "no" in the workplace, for fear you'll seem like a lightweight or slacker. Second, the interaction field is multidisciplinary and we gather a fairly broad range of skills—experimental

---

95   In fact, the best way to get an engineer to implement a feature you want is to pose it as a problem for them to solve—"I'm not sure how we could make this really fast for the user, maybe some sort of date parser? Is it even possible to do that?" They'll start pondering and maybe they'll come up with an implemented solution to the problem in a spare hour. PMs will use this trick on you, too.

design, copywriting, info architecture, HTML, JavaScript, visual design, icon hacking, and bug fixing. On small, lean teams—the types that you see at startups or at the IT departments of not-primarily-technology companies—the interaction professional is going to have to do a lot of these things. Compare to a major technology innovator like Yahoo! or Microsoft—they have a plethora of highly specific HCI-related positions like information architect, visual designer, field analyst, product designer, and UI engineer.

If your role is very well defined, you have somewhat less metawork to do. But on a team with amorphous or ill-defined roles you often have to explicitly articulate what you need from your team members. You have the right to expect PRDs from your product managers, timely tech decisions from your engineers, and that once people agree on a design, it gets built to spec in good faith.[96]

Recall the management shift that happened in the 80s and 90s, when you had to start thinking of coworkers as your "team." This means that you are all mutually obliged to one another to cover your turf to the best of your abilities. Just because the PM is near the goal doesn't mean that they're the goalie—but if they happen to be near the goal, they'd better try to stop the other team from scoring. This is great when your team is gelled, and in its dysfunctional expression can lead to busybody micromanaging between all team members.

When you're building software, there's a list of things you have to do to get the software out the door. For example, let's say that list consists of the following To-Dos:

— scheduling and resource planning
— business analyses, market research—broad trends of market segments
— end user research—concrete minute needs of individuals
— designing and planning the behavior and functionality
— building the product
— finishing & cleaning up the product
— launching / deploying the product
— supporting the product

You have to figure out who is doing what. A lot of the roles are fairly lockstep with people's academic training and conventional organizational roles: You need some sort of person qualified to make business decisions, a researcher, some customer support people, and some engineers. The best way to figure out who is doing what is to sit down at the beginning of the project and flat out say, "I can be responsible for making these decisions and collecting usability data. I need you to give me some sort of requirements document. I'll translate that into wireframes, and we'll review them, and you'll give me your approval."

If that arrangement sounds icky to the product manager, they have a chance to say so. It is very important to avoid the tendency to steamroll other team members. If the PM really, really thinks he should have a role in creating wireframes, you will make your lives miserable by sweeping that under the rug. If you decree that you get to do all the wireframes and the PM is not to be involved, the PM will feel marginalized and will have a latent bitterness at not getting to have sufficient say. If you're lucky he'll be passive aggressive and nitpick you to death during review meetings until

96 (Not "Oh, I thought you wanted to button text to say 'Lorem Ipsum', and now it's in the hands of QA, so sorry, too late.")

the wireframes are what he would have done. If you're unlucky he'll ignore your work, do his own, and talk it over with the engineering team behind your back, and get them to implement his version ("Oh, it was faster that way. Don't worry, we'll test it, and if it doesn't work we can change it.")

It is difficult to be direct and say to the PM, "I want to see your wireframes because those are an important way for me to understand your requirements and your thoughts, but let me produce the final deliverable." This has the added bonus of pointing out that you're going to be doing the dirty work of producing and maintaining the design spec.

If you have a PM who comes from an HCI background, you'll have more overlap and therefore more potential conflict. For example, I work best with the business-analyst type of PM: someone who's keen on figuring out the product in the rest of the organization and giving me market goals. They don't need to have the interaction vision in their head; they focus on the strategic vision and leave the implementation to the professionals.

Even as a relatively junior designer in my second job out of school, the product manager (an MBA with 8 years of experience) gave me the latitude to design and deliver the UI. It was one of the few pieces of enterprise software in existence that its users could actually deal with.[97]

The interface designer is generally the person who designs the literal user interface: the screens, the buttons, the links. This is an important part of the discipline: it's the actual finishing of the house and construction of the garment, to use metaphors from other design fields.

But you can't be a brilliant designer of user interfaces unless you have a grip on the design and function of the system as a whole. That is, unless you are also a designer of experience. Sure, I can write a more thoughtful and functional credit card input form than any I've ever seen deployed in my life (and I do a LOT of shopping on the internet), but the fact that I chose a self-correcting text field instead of a dropdown for the month and year is going to make very little difference if the overall system isn't designed in a humane way. Maybe what the person really needed right then wasn't a place to input their credit card information, but a Flash movie explaining the thing they're about to buy.

Most of the designers that I am connected to through school or work are trained to be product designers, user experience architects, or Interaction Designers. The work that we're good at doing and the work that we should be doing is a superset of "User Interface Designer." My passion for what I do is grounded in making technology suck less for people. It is not for creating webpages—although that is my current medium and I have a lot of respect for it. To the extent that I'm stuck designing webpages in a vacuum separated from a holistic design of the total system, I'm frustrated. We cannot do our best work, as trained in current best practices of design and HCI, unless we can affect the system as a whole and the user experience in its entirety.

<hr>

97 Oracle, I'm sorry, I know you brag about your usability labs, but each of the products that I've used ha been miserable, frustrating, time-wasting, ugly, and unpleasant nightmares. I am a trained User Interface Designer and I can barely figure out how to schedule a meeting in CorporateTime's web application—and when I do, it is such a slow process that I almost fall asleep with the frustration of waiting for each freaking pageload. Also: beige? Come on. Beige is the elevator music of colors and you know it.

When you are understanding boundaries and skill sets, also consider the people who do the most minute bits of interface implementation. Interface coders are on the line between human and machine. They *are* the line. Gmail, 37Signal's Basecamp, and Flicker are some of the most obvious recent web products whose UI engineering played a huge role in improving the user experience. Take Gmail: it is nearly ubiquitously praised for its fluidity, in addition to its beauty, interface, and featureset. It took years of coding and polish to make everything feel that fluid. The UI coders are just as vital to the success of the project as the high-level designer. Treat them well. That kind of person often makes a fantastic teammate for a very interface-oriented product manager who loves to do flows, or for an information architect who is less detail-oriented. The UI programmer gets a lot of latitude to make minute decisions about onClick versus onMouseover; if you care about that and you're working with someone else who does, understand that you are going to spend more time in intense discussions with this person about the best way to get the job done.

This isn't a prima facie bad thing: but if you're expecting to hand off a spec and get it implemented with no questions asked, you're going to be disappointed. This individual cares about their job and takes pride in their work, and just as you strive to make the best decisions according to your professional capacity, so will they. You will have to answer their questions, particularly if you want them to go the extra mile to make the UI spit-polish perfect. Moreover: they may see it as their job to figure out whether it should be onMouseover or onClick and might resent you for trying to over-specify.

One of the other dangers when you collaborate closely with someone who has overlapping skills is that you can end up compromising too much just to get a decision made: this person really wants the picture on the left, you think it should be on the right, so you say "let's do half and half," or "let's put it in the middle." It's not that this automatically creates a bad design decision, but it does mean that the decision-making process is not based on product and user needs—it's based on the political expediency of getting things done. (Every product I've ever worked on that had this design-by-committee problem ended up a mess until all the competing principals buggered off and let one person pull everything back into a single holistic design vision.) Again, it can be helpful to set a ground rule up front: the designer provides recommendations and only in rare super-crucial cases do you set absolute requirements for implementation. Not only do you create a sort of constitution for decision-making on the project, but you also tell each other "it's okay to have discussions about our working style." You're all (probably) working towards the same goal—getting the product launched—so adjust your working styles as needed. The work habits are in service of the ultimate goal: do not make the goal bend to the will of the habits.

So the point is, you have to know your passion and figure out the types of people whose own contours give you the space to do your best work. If you overlap, you will have to take extra care to work together in a way that doesn't make you hate each other or feel like you in each other's faces. And if you want to change your focus or learn something new, you'll need to work with the appropriate person: they'll challenge you.

Changing roles or expanding your role takes work. There are two obvious ways to do this. Suppose you want to have more of a role in doing early-stage fieldwork. You need to demonstrate your level of competence so managers and coworkers know what they can trust you to do. So you can either do your fieldwork for a noncrucial project, like an internal project, or apprentice with an experienced field researcher.

If no one in your organization is currently conducting field research, you're going to have to go out on a limb. You're going to have to make time or take extra time in the mornings and evenings. Skip your daily news surf for a week and spend an hour a day doing phone interviews. Hand out PostIt notes in a meeting and get team members involved in a participatory design exercise to brainstorm principles and anti-principles.

Bureaucracy versus politics

Two people are a relationship; three people are politics. Politics are the inevitable outcome of humans, primates, interacting with one another. We say "politics" with derision when these personal relationships—which create the foundations of preference, hierarchy, and prioritization—cause us to make organizational decisions that are not actually in our best interests as defined by an objective, industrialized, data-driven process.

Undoubtedly we need to have structures in place to enable decisions: where do resources get allocated? Whose project gets the homepage promo? Who gets multiple UI designers, full product support, tech writers, usability tests, marketing resources, in addition to engineering support? When will this product launch?

Politics is a way to solve problems, support decisions, and secure resources. Bureaucracy is also a way to solve problems, support decisions, and secure resources. Some cultures (whether corporate or governmental) use politics to meet these needs, and other cultures use bureaucracy. Or, more accurately, most cultures are somewhere on the spectrum between the two extremes.

I don't deride politics per se. Politics inevitably exist; we can't help ourselves; we're only human and it's our nature. Bureaucracy is the antidote and also its own poison. You could be filling out forms in triplicate; writing 800-page SEI product specs before doing any work and getting those signed off by everyone in eng and management.

Agile software development and XP are more flexible processes that developed in response to overly bureaucratic corporate structures that got in the way of good product development.[98]

I would surmise that upper management (and perhaps each of us) needs the greatest flexibility to make decisions whenever a decision might be appropriate. And I can see why: we each have to trust our gut, and if it's a week before launch and the product doesn't work, doesn't fit the vision, or looks icky, you can't launch it simply because the Is and Ts of formal procedure have been dotted and crossed. You have to call a spade a spade and say "no, we can't launch that, this stuff has to be fixed."

At a small company where everyone can talk to one another, it's effective to use politics (that is: informal social like human interactions) and the flexibility is great. But at a company of a few thousand people, whether you can get someone's ear might depend largely on whether you've

---

98 Think Office Space. Think government job. Yuck. On the other hand, zero procedural structures turns us into Melrose Place.

known them for 5 years already; are friends with their admin; are an expert on their project. This is not inherently dysfunctional. It's a natural tendency to leverage whatever resources you have available and the simple nature of team-gel and longstanding business relations means that some people are going to have better access to knowledge resources than others.

Google tries to flatten this access disparity with an open-knowledge corporate culture. However, the solution obviously doesn't scale. At some point, the employees can no longer each give their time to all others. People start making harder choices about who gets their energy. Additionally, the nature of human interactions suggests that people who have seniority, are more flamboyant, and/or are more demanding will tend to command more attention: the squeaky wheel gets the grease.

I surmise that businesses use bureaucracy to flatten natural disparities of connectedness. However, these bureaucratic structures often try to eliminate politics. You don't get approval by stopping by the boss's office; instead, you have to fill out a proposal in triplicate, submit it to the boss's admin, and wait for the committee to review your proposal. Bureaucracies act under the premise that politics can be eradicated from the organization. So instead of getting attention or code or a UI because you, say, worked with the designer on a previous project and they'll do you a favor, your access to these human resources is dictated by going to a meeting, getting on the agenda, requesting the resources, and getting the manager to sign their approval. The problem with bureaucracy is that it doesn't get rid of politics. Nothing does. You can't eliminate human interactions from anything involving humans. Perhaps the best approach is to use bureaucratic and political systems in tandem to shore up the others' weaknesses, although I don't have a great sense of how you'd do this on an institutional level.

Intuition and the art of design

Several years ago, I was snowboarding with some friends, one of whom was taking his first lesson that day. I had stopped by to say hello to him and another experienced pal joined us. The beginner, as per standard operating procedure, was falling every three feet. Our other friend started to try to explain snowboarding according to the principles of physics involved: being a math major from MIT plus a black belt in aikido, he was more qualified to explain the physics of motion than your average person. He started instructing: "lean back, then forward, as the edge turns and catches you shift your weight..."

Our beginner friend tried to follow these instructions, getting more frustrated by the minute. I interrupted the erstwhile instructor.

"Mike, what you need to do is stop thinking about it, keep practicing, fall about a million times, and feel what it's like each time. Then you'll understand how to snowboard."

He needed to develop what we call muscle memory—an intuitive, subconscious cognitive ability to maintain and adjust his balance with muscle control in this new medium.

There's a buzz in the Valley these days that design should be a science, not an art. And indeed, in the HCI community a great deal of effort has gone into, shall I say, mathematizing usability and design work. Vividence did a fantastic job of extracting comprehensive data from sophisticated clicktracking, timestamping, and integrated survey questions. Eye trackers are similarly powerful. You get precise data about where people's eyeballs went; although it doesn't tell a complete story, it's still a rich one. You learn where people's eyes fall and how a visual design draws eyeballs across a page.

Any web-based company will be as smart as it can afford on its log analysis, clicktracking, and similar. You can see trends in how users click and navigate through your site, and particularly when they begin by searching, their motive is often quite clear. If someone goes to Amazon.com and types "gift for 5 year old," you do gain a sense of what they're looking for, and you can recreate the story of their thoughts and choices by simply tracing where they clicked at what times.

This, of course, fails quite a lot.

Did that incomprehensible click on "View this page in Japanese" actually indicate that the user wanted to switch to the Japanese interface, or did the FedEx guy ring the bell, the dog barked, their hand twitched, and they accidentally clicked on the link? Did someone abandon their shopping cart because they changed their mind about the purchase, or because they never had any intention of making the purchase but wanted to see how much those 3 items would cost?

All of the designers I've discussed this with think that it's bollocks to try to reduce design to a science. This is precisely the point Malcolm Gladwell makes in the introduction to *Blink*, as he discusses the Getty museum's decision to purchase a rare statue for $10 million. It was an unusually well-preserved specimen of a particular style of ancient Greek statuary, called a kouros. The Getty spent a massive amount of energy analyzing the statue: geological samples, a zillion types of x-rays, chemical tests, you name it. The cinch was a layer of calcite on the statue's surface, a chemical change that could only have happened to the statue's marble after many hundreds of years. The statue definitely wasn't a fake. Science had proved such.

Proud of their find, Gladwell reports that the Getty curators showed the statue to a few art historians and experts in ancient Greek statuary. Every single one of those experts instinctively thought something was wrong. So the Getty shipped it to Greece where more historians took a look.

Gladwell cites comments from historians like "Anyone who has ever seen a sculpture coming out of the ground… could tell that that thing has never been in the ground," and their feelings of "intuitive repulsion" towards the statue. [99]

Turns out that the statue was, after all, a fake. The experts' intuitions told them in 30 seconds what it had taken the Getty 14 months to wrongly prove with science.

This does not mean that science is bad. But our methods of measurement are currently too gross to give us perfect answers with true accuracy. And much of science still relies on intuition and hunches; your ability to make creative leaps depends on the sum of your previous experience. In the case of Gladwell's statue, the examining scientist later learned that the aged marble can be faked with a type of mold. Since he did not initially realize this was a possibility, it of course did not occur to him to test for this contingency.

Testing user interface is as complex and multivariate as testing the effect of a new medicine: and like getting a new drug approved by the FDA, true scientific validity would take years to establish. True scientific validity in HCI is not possible. It takes too long for too little return. I see UI being tested as science without the benefit of intuition and I shake my

....

99 Gladwell, Malcolm. *Blink: The Power of Thinking Without Thinking.* Little, Brown, 2005.

head in amazement at the realm of knowledge the scientists are denying themselves, even as they take vastly longer to reach the obvious conclusions. You may be able to measure the effect of a change in font size on sale fall through, but you won't understand why. A moderately proficient HCI professional could quickly explain visual scanning processes and the likely effect on user behavior and rhetorical effect that would happen with the change.[100]

It is easy to think that design is a science when you have at your disposal an army of engineers and analysts obligated to do what you tell them, a flexible and massive budget, the ability to set your own launch dates, and millions of users. If you operate without any of these constraints that are fundamental to other businesses, you can attempt to quantify the effect of every byte change if you want. But don't delude yourself that this is process innovation. It's a waste of time, money, and effort, because this expenditure is what at least 20 years of software process innovation has been trying to reduce.

At the CHI conference in 2004, a team of researchers from IBM presented results of a two-year study they had conducted on email.[101] They suggested that email needed some major changes, core amongst which were instant account-wide search; threaded conversations; message excerpts to summarize content; labels instead of folders;[102] and removing messages from view. It was a tightly conducted research project.

But ironically, just a couple of weeks before, Google had launched the Gmail Beta. The Gmail team had reached the same conclusions that the IBM team did, as evidenced by the featureset that they launched with—except the Gmail team made most of those core decisions intuitively without conventional field research. (Email does happen to be one of those lucky cases where the developers are some users—not "the" users, but some of them.) While IBM was running their research project, Gmail got built and deployed.

The first thing you learn as an Interaction Designer is that you are not the user and you must never ever trust your assumptions. Like the rules about never beginning a sentence with a conjunction or ending one with a preposition, this stricture is at once both our golden rule and a pile of crap. I had a terrific professor at CMU, Randy Pausch. Randy had done a lot of work with Disney at its entertainment parks. He taught a class in rapid prototyping and usability-based iteration. Each project would require five rounds of user tests with five users each, and the consequent design iterations. The class was all about learning to trust user testing and nothing but. Data! Data! Put it in front of real people! I would sit at bus stops in Pittsburgh and accost the natives; occasionally I would take my prototype to a bar on a weekend night, figuring that if a drunk could use it in the dark,

---

100 Caveat: when you work at a web-based company, due diligence CYA is probably a sufficiently good reason to precede major changes with click through studies. But know its limitations and know why you're doing it: validation, not inspiration.

101 *ReMail: A Reinvented Email.* Steven L. Rohall, Dan Gruen, Paul Moody, Martin Wattenberg, Mia Stern, Bernard Kerr, Bob Stachel, Kushal Dave, Robert Armes, Eric Wilcox. IBM T.J.Watson Research Center, Cambridge, MA 02142 USA.

102 The IBM team used the term "collections"—but the concept is that a message can live in more than one collection, the way Gmail labels work, instead of belonging to only one folder.

anyone could.[103] A few rounds of this and the point got through—real people surprise you in ways you never ever could have imagined. And thus: design decisions should be based on observed behavior, not your intuition.

We'd often have to bring in the first draft of our design for feedback and status checks. At the beginning of the semester, Randy would look at our designs and say things like "okay, great, I'm looking forward to seeing your usability results" in the kind of voice that you'd say "wow, good luck with that," when your friend tells you she's going to build a gigantic birdseed sculpture on a free-range chicken farm.

And so as the semester wore on I came to suspect that Randy could foretell every single usability problem that each of us was going to find with our projects. After class one day I stayed to ask him a couple of questions about my project. He said, "yeah, you're probably going to hit usability issues with this, that, and this other thing over here." Sure enough, each of those problems turned up in my tests. In class we started asking him, casually: what did he think we'd find? He'd spit out a bunch of issues and sure enough, you'd test your design and people would screw up in exactly the ways he had predicted.

You sly bastard, I thought. You know exactly what's going to happen without testing.

Maybe it was because he'd taught the class before and had seen lots of approaches and results to the Alarm Clock Problem. (By the way, Randy, you were right. I finally did miss a flight because of the AM/PM issue. Even better, it was with my own clock, which I've had for about 3 years and should have been an expert with.)

---

103 You should try doing this. It's funny. Use paper prototypes because spilling beer on your laptop is no fun.

Years later, after watching hundreds of usability studies, reading research, and following log experiments, I feel confident concluding: you do, in fact, learn over time. You do become a more efficient designer because you so deeply integrate humans' reactions to technology that you can start making intuitive judgments about new designs and processes. You won't always be right and you still have to test because you won't know when you're right and not, but you'll find that over time you become more accurate in predicting which designs will best solve particular problems. This means you get it right faster.

Trust your learning and knowledge. Remember that you will still be wrong, but even if you're wrong the same percentage of the time, you can spit out designs without quite so much painful deliberation and get done faster anyway.

Finger puppets, the IDEO tradition, and other UI-designer la-la land techniques

One night I was having dinner with a friend from Yahoo!—he heads up their innovation group and wrote a book on marketing a while back. He was talking about an offsite he went to with his group, which is generally made up of hardcore research scientists. He told me how funny it was to listen to them talk: algorithms, optimization, blah blah blah, and then everyone would laugh and he had no idea what the joke was.

"Someone probably said 'Don't drink and derive,' I replied.
"Yeah, no kidding." He shook his head. "They're just on a different planet. Sheesh. Engineers. No, not even engineers. Scientists."

"Yes, and you know they talk about you as 'the marketing dude,'" I said.

"Marketing whore."

"What?"

"Marketing whore. They call me the marketing whore."

Apparently every time Oliver discusses market research and tries to use this sort of data to talk to the researchers about possible venues of investigation, they scoff. Oliver of course realizes what we all realize—market and usability research usually isn't hardcore and statistically valid. But what these scientists are apparently missing is that *that's okay*. You don't necessarily find the prevalence of problem A versus B, but you do get a sense of how users approach the task and you get some catalog of what all possible problems with the system are. You may find out that one or two problems are clearly very severe and have to be fixed no matter what. But aside from that, usability problems are usually prioritized by some combination of severity and ease to fix ("Well, people kind of got this, but we can probably improve clarity by 100% if we just use a different label, so we might as well fix that—search quality is more important but that'll take three people a month and a half.").

I suggested that he just try to get them to watch the actual studies—then they will get the raw data themselves and won't feel like it's being mediated. They may make some erroneous conclusions, but at least they'll be making them, and they'll presumably make some good conclusions too in the process—and they'll get used to observing human behavior.

One of the best ways to convince people at your organization to do user research is to psych them up with IDEO's work and processes. As part of its Intro to HCI course, CMU shows a Nightline segment on IDEO's process that was done in the late 90s. It's a wakeup call. Everyone in the room perks up. They've been slogging through contextual inquiries and heuristic analyses for the past month, bickering with teammates about the deep essence of "real world—system match," and suddenly all of those techniques fall together in the hands of people who are having fun and using literary rather than statistical methods of analyses.

Designers coming from colleges like Stanford and CMU are trained in the basic methodologies that IDEO uses, with some minor differences. Specifically at CMU, students are taught a lot about the value of UI process and practice a wide range of tools and methodologies. As a designer you can yell until you're blue in the face that you shouldn't be starting with mockups instead of first doing interviews, Contextual Inquiry, information architecture, and wireframes. But until your coworkers understand why and how playing with finger puppets helps to get the software done, they will think you are a flake.

IDEO makes fantastic products partially because they spend the time to do design and they understand what design is. (And partially they're really smart and talented.) In many organizations people are skeptics about the worth of traditional design techniques, and no one believes you when you tell them that field research and finger puppets work. The unconverted tend to see early-stage design work as bureaucratic nonsense, which they will put up with so long as it doesn't slow them down or require their attention. But it does slow everyone down (apparently) because instead of immediately producing HTML, you start drawing cartoons and taking Polaroid's of people using their cell phones in grocery stores.

However, in the projects where I've actually gotten to do even slices of this type of work, I get thanks from engineers, PMs, and the rest of the team. The projects go faster and more smoothly. Decision-making gets sliced into relevant chunks and dependencies are reduced.

Spend more time up front (which saves tons of time down the road), do iterative prototyping and testing, start low-fidelity and gradually gain resolution. It's not that you can't get amazing products without it, it's just that you're more likely to consistently get well-designed task-centric products in much less time and with much less argument, stress, and strife. Team dynamics tend to improve so much with good design process that even if these processes had no temporal benefit, they'd still be worthwhile.

The moral of the story

It breaks my heart to see designers, like the housewives of *The Feminine Mystique,* slowly grow passionless and cynical about their jobs under the weight of heavy management and busybody nonexperts. When I interview people for design jobs I ask them what makes a good designer, or why they became designers. I listen for the spark of belief that design makes the world a better place: that our work is meaningful and that we can make the world a better place through care, attention, and the right decisions. It can be so terribly difficult to do this in an environment where either people don't care about making the world better, or they don't understand that your work makes that happen: that you, the designer, given the latitude to fully exercise all of the skills that you have spent years developing, are a huge contributor to positive social change. And even if no one deserves respect without first earning it, you deserve the chance to earn it.

There is room in industry, even in the smallest enterprise shop, to believe in the value of your work and make that value known to others. One of the most remarkable days of my career thus far was when a PM whom I respect said to me, "Sure, do what needs to be done. I trust you."

IN SUMMARY

This text has positioned Interaction Design in a way that emphasizes the intellectual facets of the discipline. It has discussed the role that language, argument, and rhetoric play in the design of products, services, and systems. Uday Gajendar has examined various academic approaches to thinking about Design, with the conclusion that the Designer is a liberal artist left to infuse empathy in technologically driven products. This idea of language is extended to poetry, and the text has introduced the idea of a poetic interaction—an interaction that affects not only the mind and body, but also the soul.

The text has also examined the tools and techniques used by practitioners in their day-to-day experiences. These include methods for structuring large quantities of data, and ways of thinking about users, and approaches for thinking about human behavior as it unfolds over time. The toolkit for Interaction Designers is full of methods for connecting people and data; particular software packages are incidental, as the true value Interaction Designers can provide is in their process and method. Justin Petro discussed ways in which he has used these visual tools, techniques, and methods to communicate with business leaders and with clients.

Finally, the text has introduced the idea of Interaction Design as an integral facet of the business development process. Chris Connors described the success he had working in tandem with engineers, while Ellen Beldner examined some of the trials and tribulations of working with product managers. Interaction Design, when successful, is positioned as a critical component of product development, not as some ancillary service that is called in at the end of a project.

Designers have long since bemoaned their lack of representation in industry—they claim to be misunderstood, underpaid, and relegated to stylist or pixel pusher. If Designers are, in fact, stylists, then they deserve to be paid to style: to create a temporary visual feeling that is transient and cheap. But Interaction Design is not about a transient aesthetic. A "cool flash interface" defines Interaction Design in the same way that accounting defines strategic business development—not at all. Interaction Designers are trained to observe humanity and to balance complicated ideas, and are used to thinking in opposites: large and small, conceptual and pragmatic, human and technical. This is not a jack of all trades. Instead, it is a shaper of behavior. Behavior is a large idea, and may, at first blush, seem too large to warrant a single profession. But a profession has emerged nonetheless. This professional category includes the complexity of information architecture, the anthropologic desire to understand humanity, the altruistic nature of usability engineering, and the creation of dialogue.

Human behavior is innately poetic; it is natural, and thus resonates poetic in the same way that does a flower, or a bird, or a tree. It is through our own design of objects, services, and systems that we may have disturbed the poetry. A focus on technology or aesthetics alone creates a world of ideas that often seems discretely disconnected from humanity. Through the combination of technology, aesthetics and humanity, we will find a world of Interaction Design. And Interaction Design, as the study of dialogue between people and things, will bring harmony to technological advancement.

GLOSSARY

Aesthetics

Usually used to describe visual beauty, aesthetics can be considered the analysis, study, or consideration of elements of pleasure or happiness as related to a stimulus. Aesthetics also has connections to ancient philosophy, as thinkers like Aristotle and Plato continually considered the role aesthetics plays on the soul.

Affordance

The first use of the word affordance is generally attributed to James Gibson, a psychologist researching the nature of visual perception. An affordance visually indicates how something is to be used. In design, affordance has been commonly used to indicate the physical interaction required to operate an artifact. The word now also serves to describe pixel-level visual cues found in software that indicate how to operate digital artifacts as well.

Anthropometrics

Related to Human Factors, anthropometrics refers to the physical sizes, shapes, and relationships found in the human body. The study of anthropometrics commonly implies an attempt to design for multiple body sizes and shapes, and is frequently used in the context of Universal Design.

Anthropomorphism

Anthropomorphism is the act of assigning human qualities to non-human entities. For example, one might claim that a soy sauce container "looks like a duck"; the container likely bears few pragmatic connections to a duck, but has various properties that, when taken as a whole, allude to the animal.

Biomimicry

Frequently, Designers turn to nature for inspiration. Biomimicry is the design strategy of noting the beauty and elegance found in nature and consciously applying these principles in the design process.

Brand

A brand is a level of recognition that is associated with a particular product, service, system, or company. While the brand may have a physical manifestation (such as a logo or a certain form), brand also refers to the ethereal feelings associated with the given artifact or company.

Carnegie Mellon University (CMU)

Carnegie Mellon plays an important role in the evolution of Interaction Design. The University, in Pittsburgh, Pennsylvania, offers graduate-level programming in Interaction Design, Linguistics, Cognitive Psychology, and Human Computer Interaction. The school has played host to a number of figureheads who were instrumental in the development of Interaction Design as a discipline; these include John Rheinfrank, Richard Buchanan, Shelley Evenson, Jodi Forlizzi, Craig Vogel, Herb Simon, and Allen Newell. All of the authors of this text attended CMU.

Cognitive Psychology

Cognitive Psychology is a large discipline that holds relationships to information processing, attention, learning, memory, language and language processing, and problem solving. Clearly, all of these issues are integral to the design of usable, useful, and desirable Interaction Design solutions.

Competitive Analysis

A basic technique in marketing is to assess the positive and negative aspects of products that already exist in the marketplace. This assessment, when coupled with strong usability testing and contextual research, can help to define the functional specifications that assist in product development.

Concept Map

A concept map is a diagram of the relationships between entities in a system. The visual style of the map may take many forms, but the content usually consists of nouns (entities) and verbs (relationships), with a literal connection between the two. Bubble diagrams and Web diagrams are forms of concept maps.

Contextual Inquiry

A traditional interview may ask a participant a set list of questions, and rely on the participant to remember or recall the answers to these questions. Conversely, contextual inquiry is a process that involves watching participants as they go about a task or an activity. As memories can be inaccurate, the contextual inquiry process provides a strong understanding of what *really* happens, as compared to what a user may *think* happens.

Convergent Thinking

Convergent thinking is the highly analytical process of narrowing down many choices towards the most logical and correct answer. This is an evaluative process, where ideas are judged and rejected or accepted based on some set criteria.

Critical Incident

A critical incident is an event that affects the usability of a system. Critical incidents are discovered using various forms of user testing, such as Think Aloud Protocol. A critical incident indicates that something of note—and usually unexpected—has occurred. This frequently illustrates a usability flaw.

Data, Information, Knowledge, Wisdom (DIKW)

The Data–Information–Knowledge–Wisdom chain is generally referred to in fields of Information Management or Library Sciences, and illustrates the path towards "enlightenment" that occurs through experience. DIKW is commonly referenced by Information Architects, as they attempt to wade through large quantities of data and extract relevant information to provide to a user.

Dialogue

The idea of dialogue in Design indicates that humans have a relationship with designed artifacts that extends beyond the functional. Dialogue implies a sense of longevity and a sense of experience, and serves to elevate the user to a peer level of both the artifact and of the Designer.

Divergent Thinking

Divergent Thinking is a critical part of the process of Design; it requires the rapid generation of a large and diverse quantity of ideas. During the beginning of the Design process, rapid visualization sketching is often used to generate many different solutions to the design problem. These solutions are then narrowed down through a more constrained process of convergent thinking.

Ethnography

While ethnography has formally referred to a form of anthropology that examines culture, it has been integrated into the Design process as a method of understanding people and problems associated with work. Ethnographers study cultures, and so too do Designers.

Flow

Flow is the state of focus described by artists and designers, and documented by Mihaly Csikszentmihalyi, that is necessary to produce creative work. Flow requires a total immersion and awareness of the present activity, with no regard for deadlines, no interruptions, and little awareness of oneself.

Focus Group

A focus group is a marketing technique used to gather opinions from a small set of the population about a product, service, or system. A facilitator leads the group of people through various scenarios and questions, and directs questioning towards a certain goal.

Goals, Objects, Methods, and Selection Rules (GOMS)

GOMS is a particular way of thinking about the design of software. Developed by Card, Moran, and Newell, a GOMS model attempts to break down the interaction that occurs between a user and a computer into a discrete set of steps. The time allotted to these steps can be measured, and time-on-task can be determined.

Graphical-User Interface (GUI)

A graphical-user interface describes the digital set of controls, and the methods of interacting with these controls, that the user is confronted with while using a piece of software. Traditional GUI controls include windows, icons, scrollbars, and other "widget"-style controls.

Heuristic Evaluation

A usability inspection method which compares an existing interface to a set of guidelines, or "best practices," which help to identify usability problems. This is considered a "discount usability technique" because it requires no users—only trained facilitators—and thus takes considerably less time and resources to conduct.

Human-Computer Interaction (HCI)

The field of HCI exists to understand the nature of human factors in computing. It examines issues that relate to the ways people interact with computer systems.

Human Factors

Human Factors is the field that examines the physical and cognitive performance of humans as they interact with human-made creations. The phrase is typically used synonymously with "ergonomics," as to imply a sense of reduced physical discomfort or fatigue.

Industrial Design

Industrial Design typically refers to the field responsible for the creation of mass-produced objects; however, this definition does not serve to contain the work done in the creation of system design or service design. Some choose to think of Industrial Designers as "problem solvers", rather than "form givers."

Information Architecture

Information Architecture is a relatively new discipline with roots in the fields of computer science and library science, but to call it a science itself would be much too pragmatic and would not fully acknowledge the emotional "user-centeredness" of this discipline. To be an "architect of information," one must embrace the end goal of clarity, comprehension, and creation. Ultimately, an information architect exists to make meaning out of data.

Interaction Design

Interaction Design is the creation of a dialogue between a person and a product, service or system.

Interactive Design

Interactive Design implies a focus on the technological layer that exists between a user and a piece of software or a website.

Interpretation

To interpret is to judge critically and create meaning. Interpretation is a critical aspect of the Design process; after conducting research and gathering a great deal of data, it is imperative to interpret the data to truly understand the significance of it.

Offshore Product Development

Offshoring is the process of outsourcing various services to another country, typically with a large financial incentive. While offshore manufacturing was perceived as a threat to the United States in the 1980s and 1990s, it has become a standard method of mass producing goods.

Persona

A Persona is a prototypical approximation of a target user of a system, service, or product. The Persona is intended to humanize an otherwise technologically advanced artifact; it forces the development team to consider who will be using their product, and to design for that specific user rather than for some ambiguous target audience.

Process Flow Diagram

Also known as Data Flow Diagrams or Decision Tree Diagrams, a Process Flow Diagram is traditionally used in the fields of electrical engineering and in computer science to illustrate the logical flow of data through a system. These diagrams assist in understanding the discrete rules, and their relationships to one another, that make up an activity. This analysis tool can then be shared with engineers in order to articulate and demonstrate the rationale behind design decisions.

Product Requirement Document (PRD)

A PRD is generally created by marketing to define the feature set and use cases of a product, service, or system.

Scenario

A scenario is a story used to illustrate a person using a product in pursuit of a goal. Scenarios, like Personas, are used to better understand how a new artifact will fit into the daily life of a user, and to understand the nuances of user behavior.

Semantics

Semantics is literally the study of meaning; when applied to products, it relates to the implicit meaning found in the physical and formal characteristics of an object. Product semantics are related to language, in that the form of an object and the name of that object can be inexplicably connected in memory.

Semiotics

Semiotics is, literally, the study of signs. A sign need not be a printed object, but instead can include the theoretical understanding of the process of signification. By signifying something (or signing as a verb), humans can communicate meaning, and a sign itself is thought to carry some form of meaning.

Six Sigma

Six Sigma is a quality management program that originated with Motorola; the program attempts to measure and reduce defects in the mass production of products.

Streamlining

Streamlining is the stylistic quality of designing inanimate objects that appear to be quickly moving. This technique was originally used in transportation design to reduce the amount of wind-produced drag affecting a vehicle; now, it is frequently applied to objects as a form of visual decoration.

Think Aloud Protocol

Developed by Herb Simon and Allen Newell, Think Aloud Protocol is the most common form of usability evaluation performed on software interfaces. A Think Aloud user study involves having participants use a system and vocalize what they are doing as they are doing it; the transcribed verbalization becomes the "protocol," which is then analyzed to determine where the software was problematic.

Universal Design

Universal Design is a movement that encourages the design of products so that everyone can use them, without regard for physical or age differences. Universal Design is also known as inclusive design, in that it attempts to include all humans.

Universal Modeling Language (UML)

UML is a modeling language developed to visualize the process of use cases—the set of steps that a user goes through as they attempt to achieve a goal. It is a method of moving from the narrative ambiguity of scenarios to a more formal wireframe prototype.

Usability

Usability frequently implies a level of efficiency in designed systems. A usability analysis commonly tracks number of errors or time on task, in an effort to objectify the efficiency the system affords; however, qualitative usability testing can provide insight into the more subjective aspects of product use, such as desirability or pleasure.

Use Case

A use case is a specific and designated path through an interface, usually to accomplish a goal. A test case is used by software developers to ensure bug-free code; a use-case is used by usability professionals to track the various ways of using a system.

Visual Interface Design

Visual interface design commonly refers to the aesthetic elements that make a particular interface "feel" a certain way. This includes the fonts, the colors, and the other subjective elements of the GUI.

WIMP

WIMP, or Windows, Icons, Menus, and Pointers, is a particular paradigm for interacting with computer systems. WIMP is used on both Macintosh and Windows computers, and has become the standard method of controlling software.

Xerox PARC

PARC, or the Palo Alto Research Center, was the research division of the Xerox Corporation. Many of the computer tools and standards that exist today were developed at PARC in the early seventies.

8 hardware	8 boundaries	8 speaks	7 understands	7 run	7 formed	7 sketches	7 becoming	6 affects	6 lifestyle	6 shaped
8 capabilities	8 write	8 customer	7 chair	7 shared	7 groups	7 sketching	7 full	6 combined	6 concrete	6 deep
8 components	8 resonate	8 protocol	7 phenomenon	7 inform	7 generation	7 expertise	7 complex	6 original	6 vocabulary	6 watch
8 meaningful	8 functions	8 color	7 implications	7 impact	7 developing	7 kiosk	7 deliverables	6 relative	6 appropriately	6 minutes
8 enterprise	8 insight	8 budget	7 define	7 friends	7 stakeholders	7 texts	7 click	6 finding	6 identified	6 holds
8 ambiguous	8 rationale	8 metaphor	7 limits	7 academic	7 corporations	7 helps	7 mindful	6 deeper	6 looking	6 kind
8 shapes	8 scenarios	8 theory	7 comprehension	7 albeit	7 represent	7 interpret	7 cmu	6 wall	6 further	6 artists
8 surface	8 articulate	8 plastic	7 demanding	7 constant	7 detailed	7 divergent	7 statue	6 closely	6 emotionally	6 ease
8 pretty	8 changes	8 biomimicry	7 utilize	7 organizations	7 accomplish	7 imagine	6 communicated	6 reduce	6 completing	6 menus
8 modeling	8 narrative	8 talk	7 pages	7 site	7 discussion	7 weight	6 hundreds	6 necessarily	6 year	6 showed
8 experiential	8 essence	7 goods	7 analysts	7 clarity	7 examined	7 artificial	6 capable	6 forward	6 believe	6 email
8 domain	8 step	7 integration	7 marketer	7 performance	7 cohesive	7 asked	6 interested	6 websites	6 built	6 key
8 practices	8 hidden	7 experienced	7 subjective	7 efforts	7 account	7 overall	6 equally	6 discusses	6 side	6 non
8 concepts	8 ethnography	7 consultancies	7 standard	7 mental	7 area	7 forces	6 aware	6 central	6 regular	6 increasing
8 prototyping	8 differences	7 jobs	7 conversation	7 political	7 active	7 views	6 scope	6 turning	6 programming	6 semantic
8 visualizations	8 client	7 engage	7 outside	7 opportunities	7 ensure	7 tangible	6 occurring	6 complete	6 technologically	6 running
8 setting	8 technologies	7 eye	7 discrete	7 quantity	7 predictable	7 roles	6 shaping	6 controls	6 event	6 matrix
8 generative	8 combination	7 evaluation	7 flash	7 advances	7 video	7 opinions	6 man	6 stylist	6 constrained	6 pixel